Front *of the* Class *to* Top *of the* Sales Rankings

Practical advice for college graduates starting their sales career from 35 of the top sales professionals in the world.

BRIAN CALDERONE

ISBN: 1461040841
ISBN-13: 9781461040842

To my wife, Stephanie, for always
supporting me and believing in me

To my parents, Ron and Paulette,
for providing me with a great education
and a strong foundation

TABLE OF CONTENTS

INTRODUCTION

Why are some sales professionals so much more successful than others? What makes them different and allows them to stand out from the rest? What is it specifically that makes these individuals so effective and efficient in what they do? What are their secrets to success?

For the first time, a collection of valuable advice from thirty-five of the top sales professionals in the world is available to you, as you start your sales career. The advice is based on their own sales careers, experiences, triumphs, and mistakes. This is your opportunity to be mentored by and learn from the best in the business. Follow their footsteps and start traveling on the less traveled path to extraordinary sales success and financial rewards.

This unique book is broken into chapters divided by two sections or "semesters". The first semester covers business basics. Before you can jump right into sales, it's important that you have established a solid foundation rooted in a strong work ethic and logical systems. Your previous methods of organization, time management, and communication may have suited you fine in college, but will probably not translate well to the professional world. The chapters included in the first semester cover important topics, such as interviewing, training, organization, time management, and communication.

The second semester focuses on the sales component of your job and breaks down the sales process in detail. This is your opportunity to learn from some of the best in the business on how they do what they do so well. The chapters in this semester cover sales funnels, prospecting, cold calling, objections, presentations, pricing, closing, and account management.

Top sales professionals from across the globe who have learned from their mistakes and experienced tremendous success, share their advice on all of these topics, to benefit you as you start your own sales career. This advice can be found within chapters throughout this book and in the final chapter, titled "Words of Wisdom". All of the sales leaders that appear in this book did so voluntarily to help the next generation of sales professionals. All quotes were written exclusively for this book for your benefit. Take advantage of this opportunity to learn from the best in the business and build a strong foundation for your own sales career.

To truly benefit from this advice, read this book cover to cover now and then read it again after the first six months of your sales career. At that time, reflect on the book and self evaluate to identify what you are doing well and what can be improved upon. You've selected a career that can be both challenging and rewarding. The path to sales success and financial rewards starts right now.

"Selling is the most wonderfully exhilarating, satisfying, and fulfilling career in the world - but only if you are selling successfully. Someone has to be the best - why not you?"

Jonathan Farrington
CEO of Top Sales Associates
Chairman of The Sales Corporation

FIRST SEMESTER:
BUSINESS BASICS

INTERVIEWING

The first professional sales presentations of your career will most likely be disguised as job interviews. The interviews that you must go on in order to secure a new job are actually *sales presentations*. When you are interviewing for a job, you are *selling yourself*. This is true for any type of job, where the interviewee must sell themselves and convince the interviewer that they are the right person for the job. This is even more relevant when interviewing for a sales position. The interview is the first time that your potential employer gets to evaluate how well you sell. If you can't even sell yourself, how could you possibly sell their products or services? The first step to a successful job interview is to realize that it is actually a sales presentation and to go into it with that mentality. You should be presenting, impressing, and selling yourself, as opposed to just answering generic interview questions. This will help to distinguish you from the other interviewees, who may be making the tragic mistake of viewing it as just another job interview.

"An interview is your first sale with a company. They have to buy YOU before you can sell for them. Treat them like you would any prospect."

Lynn Hidy
Founder of UpYourTeleSales.com

As with any job interview or sales presentation, you need to dress to impress. Regardless if you are male or female, you should always wear a full business suit that is stylish, clean, and pressed. Your shoes should be clean, shined, and in good condition. Your hair should be neat and stylish. Your jewelry should be conservative and minimal. Any signs of tattoos or body piercings should be concealed. If you're a male, you should wear a nice tie and be clean shaven. If you're a smoker, refrain from smoking prior to the interview to avoid smelling of stale smoke when you enter the room. Your image will set the first impression that is formed of you and will set the stage for the whole interview.

Bring a portfolio or business folder to the interview that is a neutral color (black or brown) and in good shape. Inside the folder should be a pad of paper with questions you want to ask and space to take notes. Do your homework and thoroughly research the company prior to the interview. Visit their website and learn all you can about their products, services, history, growth plans, awards, press releases, and management team. Spend some additional time researching their main competitors and familiarizing yourself with trends and developments within their industry. Use this information to compile your list of questions in advance of your interview. Include questions about the company, position, culture, products, services, competition, growth plans, and industry trends. Do *not* ask questions about compensation, benefits, vacation, holidays, lunch breaks, or dress code during a first interview. This interview is not about what the company can do for you, but about what *you can do for the company*. Remember, this is a sales presentation and you are selling to them. Several copies of your resume should also be included in your folder. They should be printed on good quality resume paper with black ink and free from wrinkles, folds, or bent corners. Your resumes are essentially your marketing materials and they need to look sharp. Be sure that an ink pen is also in your folder to take notes. Be prepared and show that you mean serious business.

Greet the interviewer with a firm handshake, direct eye contact, and a genuine smile. Thank them for the opportunity to meet and let them know that you appreciate their time without seeming desperate. Maintain good eye contact and proper posture throughout the entire interview. Speak fluently and avoid stuttering or saying "um" or "ya know". Refrain from any nervous habits, like touching your hair, rocking in your chair, or tapping your pen. Following these guidelines will help to portray confidence. You need to convince the interviewer that you are comfortable and confident in your ability to sell their products and help grow their business.

Be prepared to answer any questions about your education, experience, qualifications, skills, and traits. Anything is fair game, regardless if it is on your resume or not. Keep your answers simple and to the point, while also providing enough detail and *specific examples* to reinforce your answers. Simply answering "yes" or "no" to their questions provides no substance and makes it difficult to have a meaningful conversation. Explain how each of your answers make you the right candidate and how the *company will benefit* from adding you to their team. Refrain from long winded answers that take you off on a tangent. Remain focused and on topic at all times.

Without being disrespectful to the interviewer, you need to display that you are capable of leading a sales presentation by controlling part of the interview. Ask questions about the position, in which you know the answers could relate directly to your experience. An example would be asking if the position entails presenting to groups of people. When the interviewer says yes, let them know that you look forward to that aspect of the position since as the president of your college association you have experience presenting to groups and that you were recognized by the faculty for your presentation skills. This process shows that you know how to identify a need and then satisfy that need. It is also important to lead the end of the interview to display your closing skills. Ask the interviewer if they think you are a qualified candidate and if there is anything that would prevent you from moving forward to the next step in the interview process. Ask when a decision will be made and agree on a time to follow up with them for that decision. This technique displays that you know how to define action items to move a deal forward towards a close.

> *"Anyone new to sales or applying for a job should not forget to be themselves. No need for a 'corporate mask' or playing games. Have open, honest conversations. Know when to talk and when to shut up. Don't be needy, yet be careful about appearing over-confident. You are unique; they can't get YOU anywhere else. Don't forget it."*
>
> *Tom Batchelder*
> *Author of "Barking Up a Dead Horse"*

When the interview is over, leave your host with another firm handshake, eye contact, and smile. Let them know that you appreciate their time, you enjoyed learning more about the company and position, and that you are confident that you will be a positive addition to the team. Remind them of the agreed time to speak again and that you're looking forward to it. If you haven't already done so, ask them for one of their business cards. These are all steps that you would do at the end of an actual sales presentation. An interview is no different, as it *is* a sales presentation. Show your interviewer that you know how to close a deal like a sales professional.

After the interview, send an email or a handwritten thank you card to the interviewer and anyone else that participated in the interview. Simply thank them for their time and let them know that you are looking forward to working with them. Proactively follow up by phone or email on the day agreed by both of you to check on the status of your candidacy. Request another meeting then to move forward in the interview process and to ultimately "close the deal".

INTERVIEW PROCESS

For most companies, the interview process consists of multiple interviews with various employees, who influence the hiring decisions, within the company. The whole application and interview process is similar to the sales process, which also includes multiple steps and various decision makers. This multi-stage process is necessary to discover if it is a good fit for both parties. It allows the company to make a decision based on feedback and opinions from multiple key people to ensure consistency. It is also an opportunity for you to meet numerous people within the company to ensure that you have a good understanding of the position, company, and culture. Just as the company is trying to decide if you are right for the position, you also need to decide if the position is right for you. Will you feel engaged, challenged, satisfied, and happy with this position? Does this company provide the opportunities for development and advancement that you are seeking? Answering these questions from both sides will be necessary to find a match.

The first interview in the process is generally an opportunity to get to know each other on the surface with basic questions. It may be conducted by someone in Human Resources, as a formality, before even speaking with someone in the department that you are applying to. The goal is to screen candidates and identify those that may or may not be a good fit before proceeding with the interview process.

The second interview is typically conducted by the person hiring for the position and/or someone else in that department. The questions will be more in depth regarding your background and any related experiences. You'll need to clearly and confidently articulate details and specific examples to build credibility and reinforce your answers. This may be your final interview in the process or there could be additional steps as noted below.

The third step in the process might include a "day in the life" or an opportunity to "shadow" someone currently working in the position that you are interviewing for. This is your chance to really see what someone in that position does on a day to day basis. This should help to more clearly define the position for you and to help you decide if the position is right for you. You will have the opportunity to ask many specific questions about the position and responsibilities during this stage in the process.

The fourth step in the process may include a group interview with various people in the department of the position you are interviewing for. The group may include management, peers, veterans, and rookies. This stage in the process allows the decision maker an opportunity to receive feedback from multiple people that they respect to see if there is a consensus among the group. It is also an opportunity for you to meet additional people and ask more questions before making a decision. The third (day in the life) and fourth (group interview) steps in the process could easily be switched in order or omitted altogether.

The fifth and final interview is usually conducted by the decision maker, who you may or may not have already spoken with during the process. This is when you really need to sell yourself as the best candidate for the position, overcome any obstacles, and close the deal.

Not all interviews at all companies follow this process. Some smaller companies may only require one interview with one person, while other companies may require even more steps in the process. Some companies may complete all of these steps in one day, while others space it out over a full month. If you really want the position, it is important to stay focused, committed, and consistent throughout the whole interview process, regardless of how many steps are involved. Be "the last man standing" by closing the deal and earning the position you deserve.

TRAINING

The level of sales training available to you will vary based on the size and type of organization that you work for. Large organizations will likely have a very formal and structured sales training program. With smaller organizations, you may train directly with your sales manager or be paired up with a mentor to learn on the job. Other organizations may send you to their corporate office or outsource their training to a professional sales training company.

Take advantage of whatever sales training is available to you. Don't make the mistake of viewing training similar to the mandatory college courses that you had to get through freshman year. Sales training on the job is so much more than that and it is critical to your success. This is your opportunity to learn how to make money! Sales training is the gateway to your successful career and to a life of wealth. Just like anything in college, you will get out of it only what you put into it. The more effort you put into training, the more skills you will learn, the quicker you will find success, and the more money you will make.

Make the commitment to invest your time and energy into sales training. Arrive on time or early to any scheduled sales training sessions to show the trainer that you are serious about your career and that you respect their valuable time. Pay attention and actively participate in the sessions by asking questions, volunteering for role paying, and taking notes. Don't hesitate to ask questions if you are unclear about a topic or if you need more details or examples to make it clearer. This is the perfect time to ask those questions and to learn.

Sales training does not end when your training session is over each day. You should continue your own training then by reviewing your notes and the materials covered that day. Your trainer may also ask you to do some homework, such as reviewing new materials to prepare for the next session, studying product samples, compiling a leads list, reading a sales book, or participating in a webinar. There is no benefit for you to rush through or skip any of these exercises. They are designed to help make you a better salesperson and to make you more money. Cutting corners in training will only hurt you and your paychecks in the long run.

It won't be hard to identify the top salesperson in your office. Their name is at the top of the sales rankings and their desk is covered in awards. They have a strong presence in the office, are well respected, and probably drive the nicest car in the parking lot. This person obviously knows how to sell and is very good at it. As part of your informal sales training, you should make a point to get to know this person. Approach them with questions and ask for their advice. Watch and listen to how they do their job, how they conduct themselves, and how they manage their business. The sales leader in your office is probably the most valuable asset that you have to learn from. In most cases, they will be more than willing to help you. Just be respectful of their time and be careful not to take advantage of them. Their time is extremely valuable to them and the company.

Sales training does not end after your first month or even after your first year on the job. Even the best sales professionals in the business continue to invest into ongoing training and continuous development year after year. Take time to read books by sales experts, subscribe to sales newsletters, enroll in a sales class at the local college, or attend a seminar by a well known sales trainer. The ability to sell is a skill and the more you feed and practice that skill, the better you will be. Stay hungry for knowledge, have an open mind, and embrace new technology that can help you become a better salesperson.

> *"Make sure you are constantly working on improving your sales skills. Mastery takes time. Read books or blogs on sales, listen to pod casts, and learn from masters through webinars, teleseminars, and classes."*
>
> Lynn Hidy
> Founder of UpYourTeleSales.com

> *"If you want to remain competitive over time, you must regularly challenge yourself, challenge your sales approach, challenge your skills, and challenge your sales behaviors in your relationships with customers."*
>
> Jean Giannelli
> Managing Partner at SmartServices Network

> *"Invest a minimum of one hour per month on your own personal or professional development."*
>
> John Boyens
> Co-Founder and President of Boyens Group

ORGANIZATION

O rganization is the number one key to sales success. In order to manage a large account base and maintain a healthy sales funnel, it is absolutely necessary that you have systems in place to stay organized. Without proper organization, deals are likely to slip through the cracks, clients won't receive the attention they deserve, and sales opportunities will be missed. You will not obtain a top spot in the sales rankings and remain there without organization. Client retention and consistent sales results are the products of organized sales professionals.

If you're reading this now and thinking, "I'm a messy person that's just not good at organization", then it's time to change that. You chose to be messy (despite your mother's requests to clean your room) and you can make the choice right now to be organized. You're no longer ten years old and being told to pick up your toys at home. You're an adult now and are starting your professional career. Start off on the right foot and make the decision now to be organized. Keep your apartment a mess if you want, but at least commit to keeping your professional office space, computer, files, emails, reports, and calendar organized moving forward. Your professional career, sales success, and financial earnings depend on it.

CRM

The acronym, CRM, stands for "Customer Relationship Management", which is the most important sales tool that you will use to stay organized. CRM can be software or web-based programs used to store clients' contact information, manage schedules, track the sales process, and record communication and transaction history. If you're working for a sales based organization, chances are you will be accessing a CRM from your computer or smart phone on a daily basis.

Similar to an "online rolodex", a CRM will organize all of your clients' and prospects' contact information in a secure system. Each account has the potential of having multiple branch locations and contacts listed under the same client account umbrella. Full names, job titles, email addresses, physical addresses, office phone numbers, cell phone numbers, and more should be included for all contacts. It's also a good idea to keep notes for each contact on how to phonetically pronounce their name, when the best time is to reach them, if they prefer email or phone communication, what their favorite sports team is, the names of their kids, and other facts to help establish a strong relationship.

Ensure that you keep this information as complete and accurate as possible, so that it is a valuable resource for you and your colleagues. Multiple departments within your company may use the same CRM so that staff involved with billing, customer service, production, manufacturing, and shipping will be able to access the clients' contact information when needed. If you don't have the correct information in the CRM for the production or shipping departments, then your client may not receive the product that you sold them. Your customer service team will have difficulty providing service if the phone numbers or email addresses in the CRM are not accurate. Incomplete information in the accounts payable section could cause a delay in payment, which may also cause a delay in receiving your own commission. As you can see, cutting corners and leaving inaccurate information in the CRM can lead to a dangerous domino effect that may negatively affect you and the company. In the end, it's your client and your commission, so ensure that everything is correct in the CRM so that your client gets the service they deserve.

A CRM also allows you to record communication notes, schedule upcoming tasks, track the sales progress, and record history for each account. Every time you communicate with a client or prospect by phone, email, or in person, you should record the notes from that communication in the CRM. The CRM will automatically stamp your notes with your name and the correct date and time. Get in the habit of recording these notes *immediately* after the call or meeting took place or after you exchanged emails, while the information is still fresh in your mind. Record what was discussed and what action items were defined. You will then be able to reference these notes prior to your next call or meeting to refresh your memory, pick up where you left off last, and continue to move the relationship forward. In the beginning, it may seem easy to remember the conversations with your few prospects and clients and you may think that notes are not necessary. That will change quickly though as your sales funnel and your account list grows and becomes more complex and diversified. Keeping and reviewing these detailed notes will allow you to provide the same personalized attention to all of your prospects and clients, regardless if that list includes two or two hundred accounts.

Keep the notes brief to avoid taking too much admin time away from your valuable sales time. Simply include who you spoke with, a summary of what you discussed, and what action items were defined. An example of a note entered into a CRM after a sales call is shown below.

04/15/2011, 1:31pm, Brian: Spoke with Nick and pitched our new premier service program with 10% off for spring promotion. He's interested and will discuss it in his management team meeting next Tuesday. He asked me to call next Wednesday.

These notes will also be valuable when your colleagues need to cover your accounts for you during an absence due to an illness or vacation. They'll be able to read the history and get a better understanding of the account to provide excellent service to your valued client or possibly help to close a deal with a prospect you were working on. You work hard every day filling your sales funnel, building a strong account base, and providing excellent account management. Don't let a few days out of the office hurt your momentum or client relationships by not providing your colleagues with the information they need to cover for you effectively.

Your sales manager may run reports through your CRM to access your notes on a daily or weekly basis to stay informed of your sales progress and status of your accounts. This will allow them to stay involved, discuss accounts with you, and provide advice on ways to overcome objections that were noted. They may also periodically use the contact information to reach out to your clients to measure their satisfaction and assist in relationship building. Don't make the mistake of viewing this as micromanaging or big brother watching over you. Your sales manager is only successful if you are successful and they will want to help you. Keeping accurate notes and giving them easy access to this information will allow them to help you. You will need their assistance and advice, especially in the beginning.

For the CRM notes to be effective, they need to be well written by you first. These notes will refresh your memory before sales calls, provide valuable insight for account management, help your colleagues cover your business during your absence, and allow your sales manager to help you if they are input correctly. Ensure that you are recording notes that are timely, accurate, and detailed. As your account list gets larger over time, these notes will be a critical tool for effective account management.

In addition to organizing contact information and recording communication history, a CRM will also help to manage your schedule. After completing a sales call and recording your notes from the call, you should schedule a follow up task. This task might be to follow up on a proposal in two days, to call next week to speak to the decision maker, or to send an email in three months to measure their satisfaction with the service they just purchased from you. If the account is a prospect that you are continuing to work, then there should always be a future task scheduled with a clearly defined action item to move them through the sales process. If the account is a current client of yours, then there should always be at least one future task scheduled for that account to manage the relationship, measure their satisfaction, and seek up-sell opportunities. Schedule the follow up tasks in the CRM and then stick to the schedule. Organize your day based on the scheduled tasks that you need to complete to keep moving your business forward.

You may be able to manage your sales funnel in the CRM by assigning a status to each account. As the status changes in the sales process from cold to warm to hot, you should mark the new status in the account. You and your sales manager will then be able to run reports to easily identify your hot leads to ensure those accounts are receiving the priority attention they deserve. This also allows management to plan ahead and ensure that enough support and resources are available should the hot leads become clients in the near future.

Depending on the service you are selling and the CRM you are using, you may also be able to track sales history for each account in the CRM. This will be extremely valuable when renewing contracts or proposing an up-sell, as you will be able to easily access and use past purchase history to your advantage in the sales process. Your colleague covering for you during an absence, sales manager, or other departments will also find this information beneficial if it is all stored in one central location within the CRM. Even if your CRM does not include an application that documents sales history, you should still keep that information in a notes field within the account. Record the product or service that they purchased, the prices paid, contract renewal dates, up-sell proposals, and other critical information. Upload signed agreements and other documents if possible. The more detailed information that is kept in each account, the better positioned you will be for the next sales opportunity.

Without a CRM that includes accurate contact information, detailed notes, and scheduled tasks it will be nearly impossible to manage a large amount of accounts. The more accounts you are able to manage, the more money you will make. Don't limit your earning potential due to your inability to properly use a CRM. It is a valuable resource and is a necessary tool for all top sales professionals.

FILES

If you are not an organized person by nature, you would probably prefer that offices were still using large metal file cabinets so that an intern or office assistant could organize your files. That is likely not the case though, as most of your documents will be stored on your computer's hard drive or a shared server. You will be responsible for organizing and accessing these files. This is another situation of when organization is absolutely necessary.

Create a system of folders and sub-folders on your computer or server to store documents electronically. These folders should be easily accessible from your desktop and sorted alphabetically. The main folders should be categories of information and may include names like "clients", "sales reports", "templates", or "marketing". Within each of those main category folders, there should be more specific subfolders. For example, within the clients main folder, there should be numerous subfolders with each clients' name. Each client should have their own folder, which can house signed agreements, presentations, reports, and other relevant documents specific to that individual client.

File names of documents should follow a uniform system to easily sort files and retrieve information. Include the client name, document type, and date in the file name in a specific order. For example, if you create sales reports every week that are sent to your sales manager, each report should be saved in your "sales reports" folder. Each report should have a similar file name that follows a system like "Jones - weekly sales report - 2011.02.15". The only part of the file name that changes each week is the date at the end. When you receive documents from clients and colleagues that you need to save electronically, those should be renamed when they are saved to match your uniform system.

EMAILS

Sales professionals exchange a large volume of emails daily with prospects, clients, colleagues, and management. Without proper organization, these emails could seem very overwhelming and could reduce your productivity. It's essential that you use an email program, like Microsoft Outlook, to help organize the emails that you send and receive.

A file system, similar to the one described previously for your documents, should also be used for emails. You can create folders and subfolders within your email program to organize received emails, sent messages, drafts, and templates. Effective systems for organizing received emails are to group emails by sender or by topic, depending on your personal preference. When you are finished reading and responding to a received email, decide if you need to save it for future reference or if it can just be deleted. Simply move it to a subfolder or delete it and move on.

Don't allow your inbox to accumulate too many emails. If that happens, your responses to valued clients may be less timely, important emails may go unnoticed, and you will face an overwhelming task of getting caught up. Ensure that emails are read periodically throughout each day and that they are then replied to, deleted, or moved to a folder. Touch each email once and then get it out of your inbox.

If an email requires you to complete a task that you won't be able to accomplish immediately, leave it in your inbox as a reminder until the task is done. You can use a similar tactic if you are sending an email to someone and you want to remember to follow up to ensure they complete the task you are requesting. Simply blind copy yourself on the email and then leave it in your inbox until you receive confirmation that the task is done. If there are minimal messages in your inbox, the ones that remain will be sure to get your attention.

TIME MANAGEMENT

You made a wise decision entering the sales profession. One of the biggest benefits of a sales career is the unlimited income potential. While your friends will be working hard to impress their managers and hoping to receive a small raise each year; you will have the ability to *give yourself a raise every month*! The harder you work and the better results you produce, the more money you will earn in commissions and bonuses. *You* control how much money you earn. It's that simple. We'll discuss sales techniques later in this book to help you produce results. Before you start selling though, you need to learn how to manage your most valuable asset in your sales career - *your time.* Time is gold for sales professionals.

It's important that every minute is used in the most productive and efficient manner possible to achieve desired results. Much of sales is a numbers game, especially in the beginning for someone that is new to the profession and is still honing their skills. The more calls you make, the more sales you will close, and the more successful you will be at your new career. Your manager may share an expected ratio with you of cold calls to closes and may even break it down further into different stages in the sales process. They may tell you, for example, that on average you will need to make ten cold calls to generate one interested prospect and then you will need to present to five interested prospects to close one sale. If this were true, is there any reason why you wouldn't make as many calls as possible to obtain success? It seems simple enough, but it's amazing how many sales professionals still waste time and literally throw money out the window every day. Those trips to the water cooler, smoking breaks outside, long lunch breaks, personal phone calls, emails with your buddies, and over researching prospects online all take time away from sales calls during the work day. Those activities actually *cost you money* and limit your success. Take this lesson very seriously and start valuing your time like the gold that it is.

"All sales professionals start off with the same time. The question is not managing it, but what you do with it. As a sales professional you need to step back and figure out what activities need to be completed to deliver the desired results. Then calculate how much of your time you need to allocate to each of these activities over the course of a sales cycle (which of course demands that you know the average length of your cycle, which you may be able to manage to some degree) and then execute. As a sales professional, you need to allocate time to the right activities and manage your activities, because you can't really manage time, just what you do with it.

Tibor Shanto
Principal of Renbor Sales Solutions Inc.

HOURS

As a sales professional, the majority of your compensation should come in the form of commission and bonuses. You may receive a small base salary or hourly pay, but you should not be satisfied to earn only that amount. You chose the sales profession because you want to earn more than the average person that is paid just for their time. You are paid for your results, not for the time that it takes to produce your results. Your paycheck will reflect the sales you made, instead of the hours you worked. Your paycheck will not increase simple because you worked more hours. You need to produce more results to receive larger paychecks. If you held hourly positions before entering sales, it is time to change your line of thinking and ensure that you are not driven by the clock. It doesn't matter how many hours you work. All that matters are your results.

Do not evaluate the success of your day or week based on the hours you worked. You are not done working simply because you were in the office eight hours. Instead, set goals for yourself and evaluate your day based on achieving those results. If your goal is to contact fifty new prospects in one day, then do not leave the office until that happens. If your goal is to sell five thousand dollars in new business in one week, then do not stop working until you achieve that level of sales. The time on the clock and the number of hours worked is irrelevant and does not affect your compensation. You will only grow your business and your personal income if you achieve the goals that you set.

This does not mean that you need to work ten hours a day or seven days a week. In fact, many successful salespeople work less than the average person, yet earn much more. It simply means that you need to shift your view and start focusing on results, instead of time. The goal is then to achieve more results in less time. This is where time management skills come into play and are so critical.

DISTRACTIONS

Anything that is not related to generating a sale, building your business, advancing your skills, or helping your team is a distraction from your goal and is a waste of time. You need to take control of your day and eliminate these distractions before they start costing you money and lost opportunities.

Most email programs allow you to set how often it checks for new messages that are being received. Most people set their email programs to check every minute for new messages, so that they can receive emails right after they are sent. That does not mean that you need to check your emails every minute though. If you keep stopping to read new emails that are received while working on another task, that task will end up taking much longer than it should have. The task will probably also not be completed to the same standards as it could have been had you focused with uninterrupted attention on each thought. Make it your policy to finish the task you're working on before taking your attention away from it to respond to emails. The sales call that you're on or the proposal that you're creating for a prospect is more important that the email from Bill down the hall asking about lunch. It's still important to check emails frequently and respond timely to clients, but don't let it interfere with your sales tasks.

The phone on your desk is reserved for business calls during the work day. It is your tool to close deals and make money. Do not use that phone to call your friends, parents, significant other, or anyone else unless they are going to buy something from you. Instead of wasting ten minutes during the business day discussing your weekend plans with your friend, use that time to connect with a new client and make some money to spend on those great weekend plans. It's equally important that you limit incoming non-business calls too, as those are all distractions. Inform your friends and family in advance that you're a serious professional and that your time is valuable and ask them to only call you at work if there is an emergency that needs your immediate attention. If it is not an emergency, it can wait until after business hours.

If you work in an office and do not use your cell phone for business, then it should be *off* during the work day. If clients aren't calling you on it and you're not using it to close deals, then there is absolutely no need for it to be on at work. The only phone that you should be concerned with is the one on your desk that is used to make sales and make money. Obviously, this does not apply to outside sales professionals that are on the road and need their cell phone to conduct business and communicate with their team. Those cell phones should still be reserved for business use only during the work day to limit distractions.

If you're in inside sales and work in an office, then you will probably be closing all of your sales at your desk, using your phone or email. That means that you make money while at your desk and that you lose money when you are away from it. For that reason, it is important to limit the amount of time spent away from your desk and walking around the office. You will obviously need to leave your desk throughout the day to use the bathroom, get food, refill a drink, or attend a meeting. The secret is to minimize the amount of trips around the office by doing all of these things at once. Drop off the files at your manager's desk on your way to the bathroom and on the way back stop by the kitchen to grab your lunch and refill your water. That is a much more productive use of your time, compared to getting up each time you need to do one of these things. It will minimize the amount of time away from your desk, therefore minimizing the amount of money you are losing. It will also decrease the chances that you will get caught in office gossip or small talk, which is also a waste of time.

Most sales professionals spend a lot of time talking on the phone and therefore need to drink a lot of water. Start bringing a large bottle to work that can be filled at the water cooler only a few times a day. This will ensure that you always have water at your desk to drink in between sales calls. It will also save a lot of wasted time walking to and from the water cooler with those small plastic cups that are provided. The less trips to the water cooler, the less likely you are to get caught in those famous office water cooler conversations. Unless you work for the water company and are the one selling the water, there is no need to be standing next to the water cooler and talking during the business day.

Lunch is important, as you need those nutrients in your body to provide energy throughout the afternoon. Lunch breaks, however, are not important every day. The more time you spend on lunch breaks, the less time you are spending closing deals and making money. Instead of sitting in the cafeteria with your friends (you can't sell to them) or running errands (you're spending money, not making it), use that valuable time to advance your business. There is plenty of time after work or on weekends to run errands and get together with your friends. Bring your lunch from home (save time and money) and eat at your desk while going through emails, prospecting, putting together proposals, filling our reports, or even making sales calls. That time could also be used to eat lunch with a prospect in the sales process or to take a client out to eat. Either way, the time will be well spent in helping to grow your business. A half hour lunch break every day equals 130 hours per year! How many sales and how much money could you make in 130 hours?

> *"Lunching alone is for losers. Either have lunch with a prospect or find someone to sell to."*
>
> *Brian Jeffrey*
> *President of Salesforce Assessment Ltd*

That doesn't mean that you should never take a lunch break. Sometimes you need to step away from your work, especially if you're having a rough day, and just take some time to relax and clear your mind. That time will be well spent, as you will then return to work with a renewed sense of energy and focus to have a productive afternoon. Other times, you may take a scheduled lunch break to socialize with your colleagues outside of the work environment. That is also important, as it strengthens your bond and relationship with your team. The key is to strike a balance when deciding what to do with your lunch break. If you work five days a week and have five possible lunch breaks, you may want to consider working for three of four of them and planning something non-work related for the other days.

Smoking breaks consume a large amount of time in the work day and are often longer than they should be due to smokers chatting together. If you are a smoker, *quit now.* Not only is it bad for your health, but it is a huge waste of your money. In addition to the thousands of dollars you're spending on ciga-rettes each year, you are also preventing yourself from earning thousands more from the sales you could have made while you were smoking. For this reason, your cost of cigarettes is actually double the price you pay for them, in addition to the higher life insurance rates and medical costs you will be faced with eventually. You're not going to close any deals standing around the ash tray. You can choose to be top sales professional that earns a lot of money or a smoker that wastes a lot of money. It's really that simple.

SCHEDULES

Use Microsoft Outlook, a desk calendar, or any other calendar tool that you prefer to use to keep track of your schedule. Include events like scheduled sales calls, client appointments, sales meetings, and networking events on your schedule. Ensure that reoccurring events, like weekly sales meetings or quarterly client meetings are also listed on your schedule. Keep your schedule manageable and do not overbook. Allow enough "free time" in the day that is not scheduled with events to complete daily tasks, such as prospecting, making sales calls, account management, and responding to emails and voicemails.

Use your CRM to schedule follow up tasks for each account and then stick to the schedule. Don't allow tasks to carry over into more than one day. Skip your lunch break, stay late in the office, or work from home if necessary to ensure all tasks are completed in a timely fashion. Remember that each task is not just an item on your to do list. It is an opportunity for you to make money. Each task has a client attached to it that needs your attention, which you depend on for commission. Organize your day based on the scheduled tasks that you need to complete to keep moving your business forward.

Select blocks of time during the day for the majority of your calls to occur. The time of these blocks depends on your office hours, your territory's time zone (which may not be the same as your own time zone), if you are a morning person, scheduled meetings, etc. Select times that work best for you and for your clients.

> *"Know when you're at the top of your game (morning, afternoon, 10:00 am, etc.) and schedule your most difficult calls then."*
>
> *Lynn Hidy*
> *Founder of UpYourTeleSales.com*

Be sure to keep schedule restrictions in mind when planning your day. Clients on the east coast start and end their work days earlier than clients on the west coast. If you have a national territory, complete your calls with your east coast accounts before moving west to clients in other time zones. If any of your accounts are restaurants, be respectful and don't call them during peak lunch or dinner hours when they are busy with guests. Plan your calls for each account when it is convenient for them based on their business and their typical business office hours. Respect their time, but keep in mind that your time is just as valuable. Your success and your income are dependent on what you do with your time.

When you look at your task list for the day, prioritize the order of tasks taking into consideration your current clients' needs, prospects at different stages in the sales process, and schedule restrictions. Current clients that inquired about a concern and prospects that are at the closing stage in the sales process should always be your top two priorities. You need to provide your current clients with timely service to show that you care about them in order to retain their long term business. In addition, the prospects at the closing stage of the sales process need your timely attention to reach your own sales goals and to ensure they get past the closing stage without getting stale and cold. After focusing on those priorities, arrange the rest of your sales calls, account management, and admin tasks for the day based on potential revenue, importance, deadlines, and schedule restrictions.

REPORTS

Your sales manager may require that you submit a daily, weekly, or monthly report that includes information on your sales funnel, account management, prospecting efforts, goals, and sales results. Compiling these reports at the end of the week or month may consume a large amount of your time, as you'll need to research and try to remember information from the entire week or month. You are also likely to forget information that could be valuable to your manager and strengthen your report. Save time in the long run, by updating your report as tasks are completed. Update your sales funnel every time an account advances or falls out of the sales process. Update your goals when you achieve one of them or when you complete a task that moves you closer to that goal. Update your sales results spreadsheet every time a sale is finalized. Keep this working report in an easily accessible place on your computer, like your desktop or drafts folder in Outlook. If the report is constantly being updated, it will be more accurate and allow you to be ready at a moment's notice to meet with your sales manager.

RESEARCH

With so much information readily accessible through the Internet, it is easy to understand why some sales professionals waste large amounts of time overanalyzing and researching prospects and competition. This information may make you better positioned to close deals, but you will be closing very few deals if too much of your time is wasted preparing for the calls. You need to be disciplined and strike a balance.

It is not necessary for you to learn *everything* about *every* prospect before you call them. If you take the time to thoroughly review every prospect's website before you contact them, then you will be contacting very few prospects. Most CRMs will have numerous fields for information pertaining to each prospect. Unless your sales manager specifies otherwise, this information is not required to be completely filled in before making initial contact. This information will be filled in over time as you build a relationship and learn more about the prospect. All you really need to make the initial call is the business name and phone number. Other information, like the industry they serve and their locations, may also be helpful for that initial call. The less time that is spent preparing for each call, the more calls that will be made, allowing you to close more deals. Overanalyzing prospects' websites actually costs you money, as it prevents you from making the number of calls you need to make to be successful.

It's important to be aware of your competition and to understand their strengths and weaknesses. That knowledge will allow you to use your own company's strengths against your competitors' weakness as a proactive competitive advantage. It's also necessary to remain up to date on industry trends and developing technology, and to understand how your company and your competition are taking advantage of each. Be careful not to waste too much time overanalyzing the competition though. Every minute that you spend on your competitors' websites is a minute that you are not growing your business and competing with them.

COMMUNICATION

To be a successful sales professional, you need to be a good communicator. You are in the business of communicating with people, listening to them, talking with them, and satisfying their needs. It's important that all forms of your communication are professional at all times. This includes your telephone conversations, voicemails, emails, faxes, mail, in person meetings, office meetings, body language, and networking. It's equally important that the people you communicate with can relate to you on a professional level. You need to speak their language, at their level, to be perceived as a peer in their industry. Know the industry you serve and educate yourself on new trends and developments so that you can talk the talk. In addition to being professional and relating to your clients, you must also be genuine and likeable! People buy from people they like.

> *"The key to dealing in the C-suite is to speak their language. Imagine how difficult it is to communicate with people that do not speak your language. Avoid frustration and communication breakdowns by doing your homework and discussing issues, pains, goals, and impact in their language."*
>
> Michael J. Nick
> President and Author of ROI4Sales, Inc.

TELEPHONE CONVERSATIONS

Regardless of what type of sales you're in or what you're selling, you will probably be spending a lot of time on the telephone. It's important that you project a good phone presence and practice proper phone etiquette. Always speak loudly and clearly. Don't talk too fast or too slow. Don't stutter or ramble. It's important that you project yourself as someone that is confident, educated, and successful. People want to do business with professionals that know what they're doing. If you stutter, use too many "ums", or speak quietly, it will sound as if you are nervous and not confident in what you are selling. If you project that you aren't confident in the product or service that you're selling, how could your prospect feel confident about buying it? Sit up straight in your chair or try standing at your desk to sound lively, excited, and passionate about what you're selling. That passion and excitement will transfer through the phone and will make your sales presentation much more convincing. It will also give you more authority when leading the call and asking for the sale.

In addition to having a good phone presence, it is also important that you practice proper phone etiquette. Always introduce yourself at the beginning of each call with your full name and your business name. Give the person you are speaking with plenty of opportunities to interject comments or ask questions during the call. Be respectful and do not interrupt the person you are speaking with. *Listen* when you are not talking. Direct your full attention to the call and do not try to multi-task while you are on the phone with a prospect or client. The last thing you want your client to hear is you typing or eating on the other end of the line. Your call and your relationship will end very quickly if they think they are not important to you.

A telephone conversation should be a dialogue between two people exchanging information, instead of a lecture from you explaining why they should buy from you. No one wants a lecture and no one wants to be sold to. *Instead of selling like a salesperson, consult like a partner.* People want to do business with industry partners and consultants that are experts in their field and care about their business. Show that their business is of interest to you by asking questions about their past experiences, current situation, future goals, and growth plans. Then sit back, take notes, and let them talk! A prospect should always be talking more than you. It is your job to listen to their needs and problems and then propose a solution. If you are too busy talking about what you want to sell them, then you are not able to listen to their needs. Without identifying their need, there can be no solution, and ultimately no sale.

> *"Remember that God has given us two ears and one mouth. We should use them in that order! Successful sales professionals talk for twenty percent of the time and listen for eighty percent of the time. It's crucial for new salespeople to develop their active listening skills."*
> Jonathan Farrington
> CEO of Top Sales Associates
> Chairman of The Sales Corporation

The communication formula for a successful sales call includes four key ingredients: *follow up + present + listen + action.* Always start the call by following up on the last contact you made with the person by referring to something you discussed on the last call, a message that was left on a voicemail, or information that was exchanged via email. Then proceed to present new material or information, while explaining how this new information will benefit the person you are speaking with. After you are done sharing new information, stop talking and just listen to their reaction, feedback, questions, and concerns. End the call by defining an action item with the next step in the process. What information will be exchanged after the call and when will you speak again?

It's important that the person on the other end of the call enjoys speaking with you. You need to be perceived as someone that is friendly, genuine, and positive. It's perfectly ok to discuss non-business topics with them, but be careful not to invade their personal space or waste their time. You need to strike the balance of being their friend, while also being a professional and serious business person. Some of this balance may be determined by the industry or market you are serving. Traditionally, people in rural markets will want to take their time getting to know someone and will respond more favorably to those who take a personal approach to getting to know them before discussing business. On the other hand, people in urban markets tend to move faster and will appreciate it if you respect their time and get right to the business matter. Understanding your market and your customers' needs, and then adapting to both are necessary ingredients for successful communication.

> "A sales rep's ability to adapt to his or her environment can often mean the difference between winning and losing a deal. If a prospect is truly uncomfortable with you, what are the chances of connecting with them on any meaningful business level? Try to gauge

your prospect's willingness to share personal interests. If they are all business, then you should be too. But if they express an interest in you, maybe by asking you where you went to school, indulge them. Assuming that this exercise is idle chatter is dangerous. It may mean the world to your prospect that you were educated at their school, born in their area, or worked at the same company at some point in your career. Pragmatic salespeople understand that sales is more about how your prospects want to buy than how you should sell. This is why the most successful salespeople focus on the mentalities of the various types of prospects, such as commodity buyers and relationship buyers, instead of selling skills that are based on common sense. "

Alicia Shevetone
President and Founder of Sales Concierge

VOICEMAILS

If you're doing a lot of cold calling, you will probably be leaving a lot of voicemails. With prospects' busy schedules, gatekeepers, and caller ID, voicemails are sometimes the only way to reach a prospect. Although many of your voicemails may not be returned, they can still be an effective form of communication used to generate interest. The two components of an effective voicemail are the message and the delivery.

The message needs to identify you, establish credibility, and contain a benefit statement to generate interest. Identify yourself by clearly stating your name and company name at the *beginning and end* of the message. Leave your contact information twice for the listener's convenience. Some of the methods used to establish credibility include dropping other clients' names that you work with in their industry or mentioning something relevant about their company or industry to show that you are a knowledgeable professional. Benefit statements may include offering to save them time or money, make them money, improve their business, attract new customers, or solve a problem.

The delivery of the message relates to how you sound when you leave the message. Make sure you speak loudly and clearly. Smile when leaving the message and speak with a sense of excitement and passion. Sit up straight in your chair or even stand if it helps you exude confidence and excitement. Most voicemail systems give you the option to listen to your message after leaving it and rerecord it if necessary. Take advantage of this or leave voicemails for yourself to practice. When you listen to your message, ask yourself if you sound like someone that you would want to call back. Do you sound professional, confident, and successful? Keep in mind that your prospect may receive multiple voicemails from sales professionals during an afternoon of meetings. When they listen to all of the voicemails, will your message be the one that stands out and gets the call back?

Your own voicemail greeting (the message that people hear when they call you) should be professional and welcoming. If it is an incoming lead or a referral calling, it could be the prospect's first impression of you and it needs to be a positive one to start off the relationship on the right path. You want them to continue leaving their message, instead of hanging up and calling a different extension or calling your competitor. Make sure that you speak clearly and that there is no background noise. Simply state your name and your company's name, ask the caller to leave their message with contact info, and assure them that you will return their important call promptly.

EMAILS

Sending a business email to a potential client is very different than sending an email or text message to a friend. The email needs to be properly formatted and include correct spelling, punctuation, and grammar. Do not use abbreviations, slang, or any potentially offensive language. Always use spell check and re-read every email before sending it for quality assurance. Avoid using extensive CAPS, italics, or bolding in your emails. Stay away from unique or fun fonts and just stick to the basics fonts of Arial, Calibri, and Times New Roman. Do not use borders, background images, or colors. Emails are a form of professional communication to make money; not an opportunity to express yourself artistically. You're a sales professional; not an artist. Just keep your emails clean, conservative, and professional. Your recipient will appreciate it and view you as a serious business person.

Every email that you send should include your professional signature at the end. This signature should use the same formatting rules outlined above. Unless your company guidelines require otherwise, refrain from using any colors or images in your signature. Do not include quotes, tag-lines, or links to any non-business websites. Your signature should simply include your full name, your job title, any related accreditations you may have, your company name, your contact information, and a link to your company's website. The rest is just unnecessary clutter that distracts from your sales message.

FAXES

It is unlikely that you will be faxing much sales information to prospects and clients, as most information is now sent by email. In the instance that you do need to send a fax, make sure it is done right.

Include a cover sheet with all faxes. This should be a professionally typed document that includes your company name or logo, your name, the person's name you are sending the fax to, their fax number, the date, and the number of pages being faxed. Don't get lazy and handwrite your cover sheets. This is the first piece of information that a prospect may see from you and it's important that it is professional to help them form a positive impression. Simply create a fax cover sheet template in Word, keep it saved on your computer, and fill in the necessary information each time you need to send a fax.

Do not fax any marketing materials that have a dark background or that contain a lot of images. These color images will not transfer well to a black and white faxed image. The dark colors will blur together, which will make your information look unprofessional and difficult to read.

MAIL

Depending on the product or service that you are selling, you may need to send marketing materials, proposals, or forms through the mail. Use professional envelopes, stationary, brochures, and forms that include your company's logos and colors. Do not send any materials that are not in mint condition or that are outdated. These materials represent you and the products you are selling. It's essential that they are perfect and professional to help create a positive impression.

Enclose your business card with all mailed materials, regardless of how many times you may have shared your card with the person you are mailing it to. Your business card with mailed materials is comparable to your signature with emails or your cover sheet with faxes. They all identify you as the person supplying the information and provide your contact information to your clients.

Ensure that proper postage is used on all mailed materials to prevent any delivery delays. Most packages that include brochures, business cards, and other marketing materials will weigh more than standard letters and will cost more than a single first class stamp to mail. If possible, use FedEx or UPS overnight delivery to ensure prompt and secure delivery of important packages that contain proposals, applications, or other forms. It's critical that these forms reach your client in a timely fashion to move the sale forward without any delays or interruptions.

FACE TO FACE MEETINGS

If you are in outside sales, you will be meeting with prospects and clients face to face on a regular basis for presentations, meetings, and relationship building. Even if you are in inside sales, there may still be instances where you need to meet with prospects to close a deal or to visit clients for relationship building. Regardless of how often you are meeting with prospects or clients, the importance of these meetings does not change. It's essential that you are prepared, professional, and communicate well during these in person meetings.

Make sure that you are well prepared before every meeting with a prospect or client. Confirm the meeting time, address, and all participants. Ensure that you know how to get there and allow extra time for delays caused by traffic, construction, or weather. Bring a professional portfolio with paper and pen to take notes during the meeting. Include marketing materials, contracts, samples, or other items to aid in your sales presentation. Bring enough business cards to share with everyone that you meet with.

Wear a nice business suit *every* time you meet with a prospect or client. It doesn't matter what you are selling, what type of business you are selling to, or what the other person is wearing. You are the salesperson and you need to look professional and polished at all times. Wearing a suit conveys that you are serious about your profession and the product you are selling. It also shows that you respect the person you are meeting with and that you appreciate their time and their business. Make sure the suit is clean, pressed, stylish, and fits you correctly. Many people judge a book by its cover. Your suit is your "cover". How will you be judged and what impression will you make? Your sale may depend on it. In addition, refrain from smoking before or chewing gum during the meeting. Turn off your cell phone and remove any possible distractions.

Besides being prepared and dressing professionally, the message that you share at your meeting and how you communicate it is obviously very important. We'll talk more about the content of your sales presentation in a later chapter, but for now we're focusing on the communication aspect of the presentation. Most of the communication guidelines for a telephone conversation described earlier also apply to in person meetings. You still need to speak fluently, clearly, and loudly to convey a sense of confidence. You obviously need to respect the people you are meeting with, give them time to speak, and refrain from interrupting them. In addition, it's important to start off meetings correctly by formally introducing yourself to everyone in attendance. Give everyone a firm handshake and look them in the eyes with a smile as you shake hands. Make eye contact throughout the meeting with all attendees. Maintain proper posture by standing straight or sitting up straight in your chair. Avoid nervous gestures, such as touching your hair or face, swaying, or tapping. End the meeting with another round of firm handshakes, smiles, and eye contact.

> *"The greatest compliment a customer can pay you is to describe you as 'professional'. Don't worry about being liked - be respected. Customers do not buy from you because they like you, but rather because they are prepared to trust you. Being professional is not one thing; it is three. It is what you do, what you say, and how you present yourself."*
>
> *Jonathan Farrington*
> *CEO of Top Sales Associates*
> *Chairman of The Sales Corporation*

OFFICE MEETINGS

When you are meeting in the office with your colleagues, it is still important that you follow many of the rules just described. Even though you aren't meeting with clients, you should still act professional and communicate efficiently and effectively with your colleagues in these meetings. Make professional communication part of your regular routine, regardless of who you are meeting with and the setting it is in. The more you practice professional communication, the better you will be at it and the sooner it will become second nature for you. This professional communication will be noticed and respected by your colleagues, which will help to eventually propel you into a leadership role.

SOCIAL NETWORKING

It is equally important that you follow professional communication guidelines when using social networking websites, such as LinkedIn, facebook, myspace, or twitter. What started as pages, pictures, or groups just shared with your friends, may now also include your colleagues and clients. Before you post a picture or comment on these sites that are visible to your contacts or the public, think about who may be able to access it. Do you really want your sales manager or your clients to see pictures of you at the beach or at a party with your friends? Do you want them to read posts about the people you are dating and your weekend plans? You've worked hard to maintain a professional image with your clients and colleagues to earn their trust, respect, and business. Crossing these personal boundaries online could risk sending a mixed message to them as to who you really are.

You can still have fun outside of work and participate in social networking with your friends, but keep that separate from business contacts. You may want to use separate accounts or different social networking sites for different audiences. One suggestion would be to use LinkedIn or other professional networking sites just for professional contacts and communication. These are great resources to stay in touch with your clients and to generate leads and referrals. You can then use other social networking sites, like facebook, just for communication with your friends. Keep your facebook profile private and reserve it just for non-business friends.

SECOND SEMESTER: SALES

SALES FUNNEL

Sales organizations use the term, "sales funnel", as a metaphor to monitor the leads, prospects, and accounts that are within various stages of the sales process at any given time. To be a successful sales professional, it is essential that you understand the dynamics of a strong sales funnel and that your efforts positively impact all levels of your own sales funnel every day.

To help visualize a sales funnel, picture a tornado funnel or a funnel that you may keep in your garage to put oil in your car. It is essentially an upside down triangle, with the largest opening at the top and the smaller opening at the bottom. The idea is that all prospects go into your sales funnel at the widest point, but there is only room for a fraction of them to pass through the funnel as clients. Through the sales process, a large percentage of the prospects will be eliminated from the sales funnel based on their interest, needs, budget, competition, and other factors. The remaining prospects move down through the funnel as they advance in the sales process from a cold lead to a client.

Through the processes of qualifying prospects, identifying the decision makers, and generating initial interest, some of the prospects will move from the prospects stage into the cold stage. You must then work with the cold leads to understand their needs, position your product, overcome their initial objections, and generate interest. After you successfully indentify a need and create interest, some of those cold leads will then move into the warm category, where further presentations and negotiations with the decision makers will occur. Once a proposal or agreement is created, the warm lead moves into the hot category and is ready to buy soon. When the deal is finalized, the lead that started as a prospect at the top of your sales funnel finally emerges as a new client at the bottom of your funnel. A sample diagram of a sales funnel is shown below. Notice that this sales funnel is closed at the bottom, unlike a traditional funnel in your garage. This symbolizes that clients don't pass all the way through the funnel and go away once they sign on the dotted line. They remain in your funnel for continued account management and up-sell opportunities that you are ultimately responsible for.

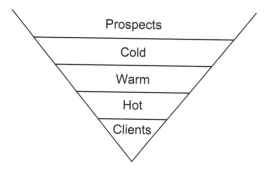

PROSPECTS

A prospect in sales is defined as any person, company, or organization that you are attempting to sell your products or services to. Prospects might include companies within your local market that you would like to sell local advertising to, Human Resources professionals within your industry that you would like to sell recruitment services to, restaurants within your defined territory that you would like to sell supplies to, or residents within a defined income bracket that you would like to sell investment or mortgage services to. They are all prequalified prospects in the very basic sense that they are located within your defined sales territory and conduct business in the industry that you serve. You may or may not have the contact information of the decision maker for prospects and you don't know yet if they even need your services. That is why they are still prospects.

The prospects section is the largest section of your sales funnel. Every time you are making a cold call or knocking on a door for the first time, you are reaching out to a new prospect that goes into your sales funnel. In order to convert a prospect into a lead within the cold section of your funnel, you must first identify the decision maker and obtain their contact information. Without that information, it is impossible to communicate with them and move that prospect further in the sales funnel. You might also generate some initial interest, share some introductory information, and better qualify the prospect at this stage.

COLD

The cold section, or the discovery stage, of your sales funnel is when the seller and the buyer are both learning about each other through questions and answers to see if there may be a fit. The goals when contacting leads in the cold section of your sales funnel is to identify their needs and generate an interest in your product. You already know who the decision maker is, but do you know what is needed to make them buy, what their budget is, what their concerns are, or if they are already a customer of your competitor? These questions, among others, will need to be answered at this stage in order to generate interest and convert a cold lead into a warm lead. Start by asking open ended questions, followed by more specific questions, and end with a trial close question. This process will help you and your prospect to understand their current situation, their immediate and future needs, and what it will take to do business together. The trial close question will help you to further qualify the prospect by gauging their interest and readiness to buy. The decision maker will likely have many questions for you too and they may want to review materials on your product or service at this stage to gain more information.

In order to move a lead from the cold section of your funnel into the warm section, you must generate interest and qualify the prospect. They must have a need and be interested in your product or service to satisfy that need. They must also be in the market to purchase your product in the near future, have the budget allocated for it, and be free of any legal limitations (contracts, laws, or age restrictions). Many leads will fall out of your sales funnel at this stage and will not advance in your funnel, due to lack of interest, needs, budget, competition, or limitations. Depending on the product or service you are selling, only a percentage of cold leads can be expected to convert into warm leads and advance further in your sales funnel.

WARM

A warm lead is typically a decision maker that has a need, is interested in your product or service, and has the budget and ability to make a purchase soon. Most warm leads have already received your sales materials in the prior stage and are now somewhat familiar with your company and what you are offering them.

This is typically the stage in the sales funnel where the sales presentation occurs. This is the time when you create value by getting into more detail on the features and benefits that you offer. You'll focus on the features and benefits that directly satisfy the prospect's need, while answering questions and overcoming any objections. This is also when recommendations are made, prices are discussed, and proposals are created. If the sales presentation is successful and a proposal has been created, then the warm lead is successfully converted into a hot lead and moves further down the sales funnel.

HOT

A hot lead is a decision maker that is ready to buy. They've learned about your product or service, you've learned about their needs, and there is a mutual interest in moving forward. This is now the closing stage of the sales process when you can finally ask for the sale and earn their business. It's when any final objections must be overcome, prices are negotiated and finalized, and contract terms are agreed to. If all goes well, an agreement will be signed and that hot lead will convert into a new client. What started as a prospect has moved all the way through your sales funnel and is now a client.

CLIENTS

This section of the sales funnel is made up of your current clients. These clients have passed through the sales funnel, have signed agreements, and are currently doing business with you. So why are they still in your sales funnel? Now that these clients have decided to start a business relationship with you, it is your responsibility to provide them with account management, ensure they are fully satisfied, prepare for contract renewals, and hopefully identify up-sell opportunities. Your relationship with your clients does not end when they reach the bottom of the sales funnel. If the relationships are mutually beneficial and are managed correctly, they will provide years of commission to you through renewals, up-sells, and referrals.

MANAGE YOUR SALES FUNNEL

A professionally managed sales funnel can accurately forecast deals and can be counted on to produce consistent results. For this to happen, all sections of the sales funnel must be full at all times. You must keep feeding the funnel at the top with prospects if you expect it to keep producing results at the bottom with sales and new clients. Don't make the common mistake of ignoring the top sections of your sales funnel, just to focus on the hot leads at the closing stage. This strategy may produce immediate results, but it will backfire with much less results following. Without enough prospects at the top of your funnel, your sections below are sure to suffer. This will produce inconsistent results, as your sales numbers ride the rollercoaster up and down each month. It's essential that you are constantly adding new prospects and moving leads through the sales funnel if you expect to maintain consistent results and grow your business with new clients.

You should update and track your own sales funnel on a daily basis as part of analyzing your business. This will help you to identify any red flags before it is too late so that you can switch your efforts to prospecting when needed to fill your funnel. It will also allow you to accurately forecast your upcoming sales, which will help you to budget and adjust your finances at home when needed. Your sales manager will also appreciate your accurate and timely forecasts, as he is asked to make team forecasts and financial decisions based on that information.

Your CRM may provide the ability to classify accounts as to what section of the sales funnel they are in. You can then easily see your full sales funnel by running a report or perhaps by viewing it on your dashboard. You can also track your own sales funnel using a spreadsheet tool like Microsoft Excel. Highlight the rows with different colors to identify the different sections of your sales funnel and then input the accounts that belong in each section. As each account moves through the sales funnel during the sales process, simply drag that cell into the correct section on your spreadsheet. You can even include additional information for each account in the other columns such as, forecasted revenue, expected sale date, locations, etc. It may make sense to only keep track of this detailed information for your warm and hot leads to avoid overcomplicating your funnel.

> *"Know your numbers and understand your sales funnel. How many active sales opportunities do you need to close one sale? How many prospects do you need to get one sales opportunity? The 'weighted value' (the gross value of the sale multiplied by the percentage chance of getting it) of the sales opportunities in your sales funnel must equal or exceed your quota or you'll never make it."*
>
> *Brian Jeffrey*
> *President of Salesforce Assessment Ltd*

PROSPECTING

Prospecting is like fishing. All of the possible clients in your territory are like all of the fish in your lake. Just as fishermen have boats, fishing poles, and bait to catch fish, you too have the tools you need to attract new clients to your business with computers, phones, marketing materials, samples, and testimonials. A professional fisherman doesn't stop fishing just because he caught fish last week. He keeps fishing for more fish day after day to supply the market and earn a living. The same is true for successful sales professionals that never stop prospecting for new leads. Make it part of your daily routine to prospect and identify new leads to call upon.

> *"Schedule a minimum of one hour each and every day dedicated to prospecting or new business development activities. Proactively plan your day and manage your time."*
>
> *John Boyens*
> *Co-Founder and President of Boyens Group*

IDENTIFYING NEW PROSPECTS

New prospects can be found anywhere and everywhere. If you're in B2B (business to business) sales and have a local territory, then many of the businesses that you drive by around town could be your prospects. Businesses that advertise in your local newspaper, yellow pages, websites, or coupon books could be your prospects. Companies running commercials on local radio or television stations are all possible prospects. Businesses running help wanted ads, sponsoring local events, or advertising on local billboards could be your prospects. You may also locate new prospects through local networking events, professional associations, and client referrals.

If you are targeting prospects within a certain industry, then you may want to use industry publications, websites, trade shows, associations, and social networking groups to help identify new prospects. Subscribe to industry publications (many are free to qualified professionals), attend the trade shows, and make the small investment to join the associations. Mailing lists and email lists of decision makers within your industry can also be purchased if you want to initiate a direct marketing campaign to these prospects.

PREPARING TO CONTACT NEW PROSPECTS

You'll need to do some minor preparation and organization before you can contact the new prospects that you identify. It is recommended that you do your prospecting during off peak hours to make the best use of prime business hours. Dedicating the last hour of your work day or spending time at night or during the weekend for prospecting is time well spent. Use that time to identify prospects, search your CRM (to ensure no one else is working them if you have a shared territory), enter their contact information into your CRM, and then schedule an open task for the day that you plan to contact them.

You may want to quickly visit the prospects' website to gather some basic information that you can add to your notes to help you with the first call. Do not waste time over analyzing and researching the prospects. Basic information, like number of locations, markets served, and business model are all that are needed at this time. Additional information will be uncovered during conversations with the prospects and are not needed at this time. You may never reach the decision maker and then all of that time researching would be a waste. Instead, use that time to locate more prospects. Sales is a numbers game and you are better off contacting more prospects that you know something about then you are contacting just a few prospects that you know everything about.

Enter all of the prospects' information into your CRM and schedule tasks to contact them all on the same day. That way, you can make numerous calls to these new prospects, back to back, without interruptions. This will allow you to strike a rhythm with your calls, which will make your opening statements and voicemails flow easier. It will also help when overcoming objections, as many of the common ones may be heard multiple times in the same session. You'll be able to use this repetition to your advantage and build upon the momentum.

USING YOUR CRM AS A PROSPECTING TOOL

In addition to locating new prospects in the market, you may also be able to use you company's CRM as a prospecting tool. It is already full of prospects entered by your current and past colleagues, which ensures that they are appropriate prospects for what you are selling. Many of the accounts even include decision makers' contact information, company facts, and historical notes on the sales process.

There may be accounts in the CRM that were being worked by your colleagues months or even years ago, but for whatever reason, they never materialized as a sale and your colleagues moved on. Perhaps the prospect didn't have the budget, decided they didn't need the product, or went forward with your competitor at the time. Perhaps your colleague didn't create value or urgency, wasn't able to overcome objections, or missed buying signals. Your colleague moved on to other prospects and hasn't revisited that account since. If you follow up and contact that prospect, you may identify any of the following scenarios:

- Their budget or needs have changed since your colleague contacted them and now they are better positioned to take advantage of your service.
- Your competitor, who they have been using, has not met their needs and they are interested in making a switch now.
- They didn't think they needed your service or fully understand the value and benefits of your service until you properly walked them through the sales process.
- Your personality and selling style allow you to better connect with the decision maker and establish trust and rapport, compared to what your colleague was able to do.
- The decision maker has changed and the new decision maker is more receptive to purchasing your product.

Before moving forward with this strategy, you'll need to comply with the guidelines your company has in place for using your CRM as a prospecting tool. You may be required to wait thirty days or longer before contacting a prospect that a colleague was working. You may also be required to get approval from your colleague or manager first. Even if it is not required, discussing the account with your colleague before you contact them is always the professional and respectful thing to do. What goes around comes around and you will appreciate that same respect when the tables are turned. Don't be afraid to employ this strategy. Sales is a competitive game and only those that are aggressive and take advantage of opportunities win in the end.

In addition to following up on accounts from your current colleagues, there may also be an opportunity to follow up on leads right after one of your colleagues leaves the sales team. Whether your colleague left by choice, due to a promotion, or because the company decided it was not a good fit anymore, there are likely to be many leads that were in the sales process at the time of separation. Your sales manager was probably aware of the hottest leads in their funnel and will likely distribute them fairly to the team. In a shared territory situation, leads in the other parts of the sales funnel may be fair game to whomever gets to them first. It could be a very good use of your time to go through the leads of your past colleague in the CRM to see what is worth following up on. Take advantage of what they already started in the sales process and use it to fill your own sales funnel. There will be a small window of opportunity, so only those sales professionals on your team that are aggressive and hungry will be able to take advantage of it. Don't feel bad about using this strategy. The prospects will appreciate that they were given the needed attention and not forgotten about during the staff transition. Your sales manager will simply be happy that someone followed through on those leads and closed the sale for the company. It's a win-win for all involved.

COLD CALLING

A "cold call" is the term used to label a call to a prospect that did *not* express an interest in your product or service first. This prospect did not contact you first or fill out a form saying they wanted to be contacted by your company. They were not referred to you by another client. Those would be considered warm leads, unlike a cold call to a cold lead where you are attempting to generate interest.

Dismiss any horror stories that you may have already heard about cold calling in sales. It really isn't that bad and it won't hurt you at all. No physical harm can come from someone saying "no", hanging up the phone on you, or shutting their door in your face. You'll survive the experience and you'll move on. If you have a fear of cold calling, you need to overcome that quickly if you plan to be successful in sales. A sales professional afraid of cold calling is equivalent to a baseball player being afraid of the ball. Both won't have successful careers and won't make any money. Make the choice now to overcome any fear you have of rejection and to be an expert at cold calling. Your success and your income depend on this simple choice.

Cold calling involves going through the open tasks in your CRM and calling the companies that you identified while prospecting, as discussed in the previous chapter. The purpose of a cold call is to identify the decision maker at each company, uncover a need, and create an interest in what you are selling to start the sales process. Start by simply making the call (it's only a phone, not a loaded gun) and asking for the decision maker. It's that easy.

IDENTIFYING THE DECISION MAKER

In most cases, you won't know the decision maker's name, but you'll know their role in the company. If you're calling a small organization, just ask for the owner or president. Even if they are not the person involved in the day to day decisions of what you are selling, they are still the ultimate decision maker for all things effecting the business, so it is still a good place to start. They can then refer you to the appropriate person below them if necessary. A smart sales professional would then start their next conversation with "I spoke with Bill (the owner) earlier and he asked that I speak with you concerning..." Are they going to ignore someone that their boss asked them to speak with?

If you're calling a large organization, you will probably need to speak with a receptionist or a "gatekeeper" first. This person is often responsible for screening calls and ensuring that the decision makers are not interrupted by uninvited and unsolicited calls. For this reason, it's important that you don't identify yourself as a salesperson when calling. There is no need to have a long conversation with the gatekeeper or tell them who you are, where you are calling from, and why you are calling unless they ask. Keep it short and simple, but always professional and respectful. Simply ask the gatekeeper for the decision maker by title or responsibility. Some examples are shown below:

- May I speak with your Director of Marketing please?
- Who would be the best person for me to speak with concerning your local advertising?
- Could you tell me who is currently managing the recruitment for your Dallas location?
- I'm trying to reach the person in your organization that is responsible for ordering office supplies. Would you mind telling me who that is and how I may reach them?

More often than not, you will then be transferred to someone's voicemail, at an attempt to screen calls. This doesn't mean that the cold call is a failure. It's the piece of information at the beginning of the voicemail greeting or in the transfer that you're seeking. Pay attention to the person's name that greets you on the voicemail or the extension that you are being transferred to. You have just successfully *identified the decision maker*! Input that information into your CRM and then use it next time you call back. Instead of identifying yourself as a salesperson when asking for the decision maker by title, on your next call you can confidently ask for them by name, as if you already have a business relationship with them. Your call is less likely to be screened if you simply ask for a specific person by name when you call.

In addition to calling the business direct to identify the decision maker, there are also numerous resources available where this information may be found. Many companies display their management team or even a full staff directory on their public website. Many industry associations publish directories that are free or available to members with this information. There are also numerous websites that provide leads with contact information for free or for a minimal fee. Social networking sites, like LinkedIn, can also help you indentify and contact the decision maker. Keep in mind, that the quickest and easiest way to locate the decision maker might just be to pick up the phone, call, and ask.

"Be clear about who your ideal customer is. Many salespeople waste a lot of time thinking they have a great prospect, but in fact they don't. It's hard to kid yourself when you have identified the characteristics (business size, location, job title) of your ideal

customer. If your prospect fits none of those character-
istics, you are kidding yourself that you are calling on
a real prospect."

Maura Schreier-Fleming
President of Best@Selling

PERSISTENCE

Persistence and patience are necessary traits required for successful cold calling. Every cold call will not lead to a live conversation.
In fact, very few cold calls will lead to live conversations. Most calls
will end with voicemails or messages with the gatekeeper. Don't
discount the value of a voicemail or message. They are often necessary and very important steps in the process of generating interest
and can be valuable if used correctly.

"Salespeople must find an empowering way to interpret
what most people would perceive as rejection. I've left
up to ten messages without receiving a return call. A
typical (some might say sane) person would decide that
the prospect is not interested. However, I cannot count
the times that I finally received a call and the prospect
said, 'Thank you for your persistence. I really ap-
preciate the idea you shared last May. Can we meet
to discuss how you can help us with this issue?' Now,
when I begin to feel discouraged, I remind myself that
every message is building a relationship."

Barbara Geraghty
Speaker, Sales Trainer, and
Author of "Visionary Selling"

If you are offered voicemail, take advantage of this opportunity to make an impact and a positive first impression with your prospect. Make sure that *every* voicemail includes a benefit statement. What do you have to say that could benefit the prospect? Why would the prospect want to call you back? Each voicemail should also include a sentence that helps to establish credibility. Refer to other clients you work with, industry associations you have in common, or recent awards that your company won to quickly establish credibility in voicemails. In addition to benefit statements and building credibility, it is also essential that you properly identify yourself in the voicemail. Clearly state your name, company name, and contact information *twice* in the email for their convenience. You need to identify yourself, establish credibility, and provide a benefit statement - all within one minute. It can be done successfully with practice.

Traditionally, response rates to first voicemails are very low. Do not expect everyone (or anyone!) to call you back after leaving them a voicemail. That doesn't mean that your voicemail was useless or that you failed. You planted a seed with that voicemail and now you'll need to nurture that seed in order to grow the relationship. After leaving your first voicemail, record it in your CRM and then set a follow up task for two business days later. (You should be logging notes in your CRM and scheduling a follow up task after *every* attempted contact. Make this a habit and don't stray from it!) Following up every other business day is recommended to provide the prospect with enough of an opportunity to respond to you without letting too much time go by that they forget about your message. Even if they are out of the office for one day or tied up in meetings for the afternoon, there is still enough time to return a call within two days if they are interested. If they don't return a call within two days, chances are that the call will never be returned. They either forgot about the message or were not interested enough to justify a return a call. Why wait ten days, lose your momentum, and delay the sales process just to determine that your call will never be returned? Follow up every other day to be professionally persistent without being annoying. The exception to this rule is if you are aware that the prospect is not in the office (away message) or if it is near a holiday when people tend to take time off from work.

Let's assume that you left a voicemail for a prospect on Monday. Assuming that you're practicing what you just learned in the last paragraph, you are scheduled in your CRM to call that prospect again on Wednesday. Hopefully you'll get lucky and reach the prospect this time. If so, explain that you are following up on the voicemail you left earlier this week and then proceed with your opening statement and questions. Odds are though, that your call the second time will end the same way the first call ended - with a voicemail. Treat this like another important step in the sales process to generate interest. Leave another voicemail, state that you are following up on the voicemail left earlier this week, and then include another benefit statement and reason to call you back.

On Friday, two days later, it is time to contact this prospect again. This time, try reaching them by email. If you don't have their email address, simply call and ask for it. It's that simple! Pretend that you already have a relationship with the prospect and that you just need to send them something or that you are having difficulty with the email transmission and you just need to confirm the address. Both scenarios will normally result in obtaining the information you are seeking. Don't identify yourself. Simply ask for help with the email address and move on. Now that you have the coveted email address, you have another vehicle to reach this prospect. Send an email to the prospect stating that you are following up on the recent voicemails, include benefit and credibility statements, and ask if they are interested in speaking with you. Don't send much more information than that, as the goal here is to just peak their interest and get a response. Keep the email just three to five sentences long. Include their name or company name and/or the words "follow up" in the subject line such as, "Follow up on voicemails for Prospect Company". Response rates from an email sent after leaving two recent voicemails are very high. It may not always be the response you are seeking, but at least it is a response that finally opens up dialogue between you and the prospect. No one wants to pick up the phone to return a voicemail and call a salesperson, but most will take a minute to respond by email, especially if they have already heard your voicemails. They know it is not a mass email or spam and that you are a live person that is trying hard to reach them.

If the prospect responds to your email and is interested, then share more information and schedule a call or meeting to have a live conversation. If they respond and say they are "all set" or not interested, respond with some questions to identify the true objection. Do they even know what you are offering yet? After exchanging a few emails, you may be able to overcome their objection and peak their interest enough to schedule a call or meeting. If the prospect does not respond to your first email though, then send them another email on Tuesday (two business days later). This time, put "Second Follow Up" in the subject and keep the email even shorter and to the point. Simply ask them if they are interested in benefitting their company using a phrase like, "Are you interested in improving your business and reducing your operating costs?" Who can say no to that?

Four contact attempts within two weeks is the minimum amount of times you should attempt to contact a prospect before moving on. Anything less than that is not effective and anything more within that short amount of time is just annoying. That doesn't mean that you need to stop at four attempts. Many sales professionals will tell you that you need at least ten attempts before live contact is made. That may be true, but you'll need to make that decision if that particular prospect is worth investing the time to chase or not. Instead of pursuing the same prospect for too long, you may want to try a different contact at the same company or use that time to contact a different prospect altogether. If you do decide to pursue the same contact further, continue by alternating every other attempt with phone calls and emails. Be careful not to harass or annoy the prospect though, as that definitely won't lead to a sale. You need to strike the balance of being pleasantly and professionally persistent, without being perceived as annoying.

> *"Persistence pays.   Be the last salesperson standing.*
> *Stay with the opportunity until the prospect buys*
> *(hopefully from you) or the opportunity dies."*
>
> *Brian Jeffrey*
> *President of Salesforce Assessment Ltd*

GATEKEEPERS

In some instances, you may not be able to reach the decision maker by phone or email. Employees may protect their leader and be given strict orders not to share their phone number or email address with anyone. The decision maker may work remotely and their private phone line or cell phone may not be shared with contacts outside of the company. All attempted communication with the decision maker must first go through the gatekeeper, who is usually their assistant or secretary. Their job, as the gatekeeper, is to protect the decision maker by screening all contacts to ensure that their time is not wasted with matters that don't directly benefit or impact the business. Only the most important and relevant communication will reach the decision maker. It is solely up to the gatekeeper to decide what information makes the cut and who gets an appointment to speak with the decision maker.

In these cases, you will actually need to *sell to the gatekeeper* before you can sell to the decision maker. You'll need to treat the gatekeeper like an important prospect and actually start the sales process with them to uncover needs, generate interest, overcome objections, and create value. They need to believe in what you are selling so that they have a reason to speak with you and go through the process before introducing you to their boss. They will need to see the value and understand the importance of what you are selling before they will share that information or schedule an appointment with the decision maker. For these reasons, you will need to engage the gatekeeper throughout the process so that they can relate to you and trust you. They need to be on your team, so that you can work together to sell your product or service to the ultimate decision maker. Treat the gatekeeper with respect, as they may be your only chance at reaching the decision maker who is needed in order to make a sale.

OPENING STATEMENTS

When you finally get a prospect live on the phone during a cold call, the first thing that you say to them is called your "opening statement". The goal of this opening statement is to catch your prospect's attention, gain their interest, and start open dialogue. To achieve this, your statement should include a benefit and a question. You should avoid small talk with new prospects in the beginning and get straight to business to let them know what you are offering and show that you are a serious professional that respects their time. Avoid asking how they are doing or making generic comments about the weather. There will be plenty of time for personal conversation later in the call and on future calls. You only have a few seconds in the beginning of a call though to generate interest and your opening statement is the tool to accomplish that goal.

> *"Business professionals often favor responding to people who offer a compelling message, as well as a call to action. When cold calling, quickly state who you are, what company you are with, offer a short, compelling statement about your product or service, and close with a call to action, such as asking for an appointment. By exuding confidence in your communications, you demonstrate that you are worthy of your prospect's attention and deserving of their time."*
>
> *Alicia Shevetone*
> *President and Founder of Sales Concierge*

Develop an opening statement that is appropriate for what you are selling and for the prospects that you are calling. You may have multiple opening statements to represent the various products or services that you sell and the types of prospects that you target. Memorize and practice all of your opening statements to ensure the delivery is smooth and professional. In many cases, your opening statement may sound a lot like your voicemails. Listen to the opening statements that top performers in your office use and adapt those to your own style.

> *"Even though you will reach more voicemails than human beings, always be prepared for a person to pick up their phone. Your opening statement and voicemail can start the same to make it easier."*
>
> Lynn Hidy
> *Founder of UpYourTeleSales.com*

INFORMATION GATHERING

In most cases, a cold call will not turn into a formal presentation on the first call. That normally occurs later in the sales process, unless you just happened to catch the right prospect with the right need at the right time. Instead, the first call is normally reserved as a time for information gathering by both parties. It is an opportunity for the prospect to ask questions about your company and the products or services that you are offering. It is also your chance to ask questions about your prospect's business, to qualify them as a possible client, and to show that you are genuinely interested in helping them. Don't mistake your questions as part of a simple fact finding mission. Instead, use this opportunity to ask powerful and insightful questions about their business that show that you are an expert in their industry. Ask questions like a consultant or an industry partner, instead of just another sales person with self serving interests. In addition, be sure to ask qualifying questions that cover their needs, budget, current vendor (your competition), interest level, and purchasing power.

You should *not* be speaking more than the prospect. It should be a conversation with both parties speaking, asking qualifying questions, and providing detailed answers. If you ask engaging and open ended questions, the prospect will talk. Just listen and take notes. This is your opportunity to learn about your prospect to uncover their needs and wounds. These needs and wounds will dictate the rest of the sales process, as you focus on how what you are offering is the solution to both. Be sure to allow the prospect plenty of opportunities to ask you questions too. That will be your chance to impress the prospect with your knowledge and generate an interest in what you are offering. Their questions will also help to identify their concerns and needs. If they are asking a question about it, it is obviously important to them.

"The best salespeople aren't the big talkers. They're the best listeners. When you're with a customer look, sound, and act like you're listening. You'll be a better salesperson when you do. When you talk, ask great questions. It's your job to guide your customers to understand they have a need, it's an important one, and they have to buy from you now. You do this through your questions. Don't tell your customer he has problems! Ask him, so he tells you them with his answers. Customers won't argue with their own data. You'll

get far fewer objections when a customer tells you he has a problem."

Maura Schreier-Fleming
President of Best@Selling

"There are two keys to a successful career in sales. The first is the ability to ask powerful, high-volume questions. True sales professionals ask questions that make their prospects scratch their head and say 'That's a good question'. It sounds simple, but most sales people ask weak, feeble questions, such as 'What will it take to get you to buy?' or 'Are you the decision maker?' The second key is to effectively position your product, service, or solution so that your prospect can clearly see how they will benefit. When you achieve this, objections and buyer resistance is virtually eliminated."

Kelley Robertson
President, Robertson Training Group & Fearless Selling

ACTION ITEMS

At the end of a cold call and every call during the sales process, it is important to clearly define and then reinforce the action items for the buyer and seller. What information will you be sending and when? What will the prospect be reading and sending you? When will you be speaking again? It is essential to properly define and reinforce the action items to keep the sales process moving forward.

"One of the most important questions in selling is 'What's next?', or if you prefer, 'Where do we go from here?' Ending each sales communication with a mutually agreed upon answer to this question ensures that progress is being made through the selling process. If the process is a good one and well executed, then progress through it leads to the results we are after. Never end a communication with a prospect without knowing what's next and the process will always keep moving forward."

David Masover
Author of "Mastering Your Sales Process"

If it is a successful cold call, the call will end with you exchanging contact information, agreeing to send marketing materials or a proposal, and scheduling another call or an in-person meeting. Always be sure to define when you will speak again and what you are sending the prospect in order to get them excited about receiving it and ensure they will actually look at it prior to the next meeting. The exception to this would be if "one call closes" are common in your industry. In that case, sending information and scheduling another appointment might not be desired or necessary.

OBJECTIONS

An objection is a concern or reason that a prospect has for not purchasing what you are selling. In most cases, an objection is not a final decision, but simply a concern or misconception that you must identify, address, and overcome to keep moving forward. Think of them as small hurdles to jump over, instead of closed doors that won't open. You may encounter objections from a prospect at any stage throughout the sales process. They are a normal part of a typical day in the sales profession and should be expected. How you react to and overcome objections will determine your ability to close sales and be successful.

> *"There is no such thing as an 'objection', just concerns on the part of the prospect. Answer the concerns and make the sale."*
>
> *Brian Jeffrey*
> *President of Salesforce Assessment Ltd*

In order to successfully overcome objections, you must be prepared by understanding and anticipating possible objections. Identify the most common objections you will face and practice ways to overcome them. This will most likely be covered in your sales training, as many of the objections will be unique to your industry or what you are selling. Your trainer or sales manager is familiar with the objections that your colleagues typically face and they can offer the best strategies to overcome them. In addition to training, take note of objections that you personally encounter in the field and learn from them. Whether you overcome them correctly or not, there is always a lesson to be learned that will help you next time you encounter a similar objection. By being prepared for objections, you can actually start inviting them to the surface to help address any issues upfront and move the sales process along quicker. This proactive approach to objections will display confidence to your prospect and will promote open communication.

> *"Closing a sale involves being able to diffuse and deflect (and often anticipate) customer objections. An objection means only that they need more information. They do not yet believe that your product or service is something that will yield a positive result, a profit, or live up to its potential."*
>
> *Carson Heady*
> *Author of "Birth of a Salesman"*

Overcoming an objection should not sound like a tense argument with both sides being defensive, arguing their points, and trying to outsmart the other. Instead, it should be a comfortable conversation filled with questions and answers from both sides. The best way to overcome an objection is to ask more questions about the objection. Start by asking questions to ensure that you (and the prospect) clearly understand the concern. Then proceed to ask more questions that address the concern, while also leading the call in the direction you want it to go. For example, if a prospect says that the warranty isn't going to work for them, respond with a question to confirm the objection, such as "Are you referring to the length of the warranty period or what it covers?" If they respond by stating that they are seeking a two year warranty compared to your standard one year warranty, you have identified the problem and can then propose a solution with an "if-then" question. Try something like, "If I am able to extend the warranty to cover two years for a limited fee, then would that make you feel more comfortable in moving forward with this purchase today?" You've uncovered the objection and proposed a solution, along with increasing the amount of your sale!

> *"Your conversations with customers don't have to be adversarial in nature or even constrained by the conflicts of interest that the traditional sales mindset and approach creates between buyers and sellers. We don't need to manipulate or push customers, nor do they have to protect themselves from us. In fact, the vast majority of customers are looking for the same thing we are - an open, honest, and straightforward conversation that is based on mutual trust and respect, and that results in the achievement of one another's success."*
>
> *Jeff Thull*
> *President and CEO of Prime Resource Group*
> *Author of "Exceptional Selling"*

Objections present opportunities to better explain a benefit and more clearly define your value proposition. Don't make the mistake of overcoming an objection and then quickly moving on. While you're on the topic, take advantage of the opportunity to elaborate on the feature that was questioned, tie it to a direct benefit, and emphasize the value and importance of that benefit.

Even if that information was covered earlier in the sales process, it can't hurt to re-emphasize the benefit, especially if your prospect didn't fully understand it and voiced an objection relating to it.

OBJECTIONS VERSUS STALLING

In addition to overcoming objections, it is equally important to properly identify the *true objection*, compared to a perceived objection or a stall. This is achieved by asking qualifying questions and really *listening* to the prospect. A prospect saying that they need to discuss the purchase with someone else, that they are too busy, that they haven't reviewed your materials, or that they aren't ready to make the decision because of an unrelated factor may not always be giving you the real objection. Perhaps the real objection is that they don't trust you (you didn't establish credibility), the price is too high (you didn't create value), or they are not the decision maker (you did not correctly identify and qualify them). You need to get past these stalling or brush off tactics to identify and overcome the true objections before a sale can be made.

A stall is not the same as an objection. Typical stalling tactics that you may encounter include prospects telling you they are too busy and don't have time to talk with you or review your materials. In most cases, their schedule is being used as a stall to hide the fact that they are just not interested or that they don't perceive a value in what you are offering. The reality is that they manage their own schedule each day and they determine what tasks get done based on the priority and urgency that they perceive is associated with those tasks. They need to *choose* to make time for you. Your job is to identify a need, explain the benefits and value, and then create a sense of urgency to be included in their schedule and prevent stalling in the sales process.

When a prospect gives you the schedule objection, the first step is to realize what is happening (stalling) and to evaluate your last conversation with the prospect to see what went wrong and how you can learn from your mistake in the future. The second step is to get past the current stall to uncover the true objection. Tell them that you respect that their time is valuable and then proceed to ask a question related to the benefit you are offering. For example, if you are selling advertising in a seasonal issue of a magazine, say something similar to, "I understand that you are busy and respect your time, but are you still interested in having exposure in our special fall issue that is distributed to 80,000 local residents along with distribution at 25 local events next month? If so, we need to finalize your advertising plans this week to meet the print deadline." That response allows you to measure their interest level, while also reinforcing the benefit (exposure to their target audience) and creating urgency (meeting the print deadline). It demonstrates that you care about them, as they had expressed an interest in that magazine and you don't want them to miss the deadline and the unique opportunity. Responses tailored in that fashion will typically invite the response you are seeking and you will find that your prospect's busy schedule magically opens up with time to talk.

Ask questions needed to get past the stall by identifying the true objection fueling the stall and then proceed to overcome the objection. It's as simple as identifying the objection and proposing a solution every time.

PRESENTATIONS

A sales presentation for sales professionals is equivalent to game night for professional basketball players. It's when you finally get to use all of your sales skills and product knowledge. It's what you prepare and practice for in sales training and role playing, but this time it is real. You'll have to think quickly and smartly on your feet. It is your chance to perform, impress, and win.

Depending on what you are selling, your business model, and the prospect involved, your sales presentations may be done by phone, by webcam, or in person. All three presentations have their place in the sales profession and can be effective if done correctly. It's important to understand the differences between the different types of sales presentations and use those differences to your advantage to deliver the best sales presentation possible.

The advantages of presentations by phone include no travel time or expenses, you can complete more presentations in less time, you are in your own controlled environment, and you can wear comfortable clothing (depending on your employer's dress code). The advantages of presentations in person include being able to connect with the prospect and keep their attention through eye contact, the ability to read their body language, lower no show rates (it's harder for a prospect to skip your presentation if you are standing in their office), and the ability to display presentation materials and sample products. For sales that don't involve big purchases, product demos, or relationship building and don't justify the cost of travel, the telephone may be just the perfect vehicle for closing the deal. For other types of sales, in person meetings may be necessary to get the job done and build a solid foundation for the business relationship.

PRESENTATIONS BY PHONE

If you're working in inside sales or telesales, or if you have a national territory, chances are most of your sales presentations will be conducted via the telephone. This is an effective vehicle for making sales, especially transactional sales with lower dollar amounts and shorter sales cycles. Billions of dollars are spent each year by consumers and businesses agreeing to make purchases through the telephone. It's a proven tool and it works.

When presenting by phone, ensure that you are using a reliable telephone with good voice quality. Speak clearly and do not use speakerphone for presentations. Remove all distractions and possible interruptions to ensure that you are focused. Close your office door or put a sign on your cubicle to let your coworkers know that you are on an important sales call. Stand during the presentation. This will provide you with more self confidence and will help to project more energy and enthusiasm in your voice. Don't be concerned with what your colleagues may think when they see you standing at your desk. They'll all be standing at their desks too once they see your results!

Ensure that all participants are formerly introduced in the beginning of the call. Make note of who is on the call and their role in the decision making process. Address them by name during the presentation to make the dialogue more personal. Since you can't see a prospect raise their hand or try to speak, be sure to pause often when speaking and allow plenty of opportunities for the prospects to interject comments or ask questions. Although it is a presentation, it still needs to be a two way conversation, opposed to a lecture with a long monologue from you. You'll lose their attention fast with a monologue on the phone. You need to keep them talking and engaged.

PRESENTATIONS BY WEBCAM

Thanks to modern technology, many inside sales professionals are now using webcams to enhance telephone presentations and virtually interact with prospects hundreds of miles away. This provides all of the benefits of a telephone presentation, with the added benefits of being able to see each other and read body language. It's not the same as actually shaking hands and looking in their eyes, but it is still an effective tool to help bridge the distance gap.

Much of the advice just described for telephone presentations also applies to presentations by webcam. The exceptions would be standing (you need to sit still in front of your webcam) and speakerphone. Don't hold a telephone while on camera. Either get a headset or use a quality speakerphone to maintain a professional appearance. If you choose a speakerphone, be sure to be in an office space that is free from background noise and that has the windows shut to block traffic and other outdoor noises. Your background also needs to be professional. Ensure that the area in view of the camera is clean and professional, your coworkers can't walk behind you on camera (unprofessional and distracting), and a window isn't behind you (the light will create a shadow).

When you're on webcam, you'll need to look *at the camera* for the entire presentation. This may be difficult, as you'll naturally want to watch yourself and the other participants on the screen. Although you may be watching them on the screen, you are actually looking away from the camera, so to them it appears that you are looking elsewhere. If your camera is on top of your computer, like most laptops with built in cameras, then when you watch the screen it appears to the participants that you are looking down. This will give the wrong impression that you are not confident or prepared and are reading from notes. Just as eye contact is important when meeting face to face, it is equally important by webcam, but is only achieved by *not* looking in their eyes.

You need to be dressed professionally (from the chest up if you are sitting) whenever presenting by webcam. Your attire and personal grooming are extremely important when on webcam. If you were meeting in person, the participants would likely be looking in your eyes most of the time. It would be inappropriate and uncomfortable if they stared at any other part of your body. However, when you're on camera, they can easily stare at you and may notice if your tie is crooked, if you didn't shave, or if you are revealing too much with your top unbuttoned. Prepare for a webcam presentation as if you were getting headshots taken. Your hair, makeup, grooming, and attire should be presentable and professional.

There are many programs available now, such as WebEx and GoToMeeting, which allow you to schedule web meetings that incorporate webcams. These programs make it possible to share your desktop, documents, and web pages with your prospects over the Internet during a sales presentation. Using this technology, you can lead a PowerPoint presentation or demo a computer program or website during your presentation. Depending on what you are selling, this technology could be a very effective visual aid to help in the sales process.

Invest in a quality webcam and test it with coworkers a few times before using it with a prospect to ensure that the hardware and software work well and that the lighting and sound are acceptable.

PRESENTATIONS IN PERSON

Sales presentations conducted in person are very different from those conducted over the telephone or webcam. You have many advantages in person, like being able to look the prospect in the eyes, read their body language, hold their attention (or see if you lost it), and physically show them samples, demos, and marketing materials. The introduction part of the presentation is also much more effective in person, as you can shake everyone's hands, look them in the eyes, and put faces to names. The meeting may be longer in person than it would be by phone. This is good, as you will have their attention for more time to build a relationship and help influence their decision. You will also need to really know your stuff, as you will cover more material, be asked more questions, and need to think quickly on your feet without any cheat sheets that may normally hang on the wall of your cubicle. You will need to be well prepared.

In person presentations also provide the opportunity to use visual aids to support your presentation and emphasize some of your key points. This includes product samples, printed marketing materials, demonstrations, videos, and PowerPoint presentations on a large screen. These visual aids add another valuable dimension to the presentation, which is not possible through telephone presentations. Take advantage of this opportunity, but do not rely solely on these visual aids. You are the sales professional and you are the one responsible for leading the presentation. You still need to be well prepared and able to deliver a thorough and impactful presentation, with or without the visual aids. A PowerPoint presentation can be a very effective visual aid. It will allow you to emphasize important points, while also displaying photos, images, and graphs. It will also allow prospects to follow along with the presentation, while you use it as an outline. It is important to understand that a PowerPoint presentation is *not a script*. It should contain minimal text and just emphasize key points, which you should then be able to elaborate on and explain. Do not face the screen and do not read from the slides. Keep your slides clean, simple, and professional. Busy slides with too many colors or moving parts are distracting and take away from your message.

Any marketing materials that you choose to distribute should be in good shape (no wrinkles or folded corners), up to date, and professionally designed and printed. Include your business card with all marketing materials, even if you exchange them during the meeting. If the prospect is reading your marketing materials three weeks from the meeting or if they pass it on to someone else and they have a question, they'll be able to reference your attached business card to easily locate your contact information.

A professional appearance and a positive first impression are crucial for in person sales presentations. A poor first impression could ruin your entire presentation and cost you the sale. Dress to impress by always wearing a full business suit for all sales presentations. The suit should be clean, pressed, and in good condition. Your shoes should also be shined and presentable. Your wardrobe and your hairstyle should be stylish, conservative, and professional. You should hide tattoos, remove piercings (two earrings per ear maximum for females is acceptable), and remove excessive jewelry. These accents are distracting during a presentation and could actually offend your prospect. Don't take the chance of negatively affecting the sale. Until you have established a strong relationship, it is always safer to dress and act as conservative as possible. Know your audience though, as some of the advice in this paragraph may not hold true for all products and all industries. You need to understand what is important to your customers and how to relate to them. For example, if you are selling products to tattoo parlors and your prospects are tattoo artists, then dressing casual and showing your own tattoos could actually help your chances of earning their business by relating to them and establishing credibility. Be aware of the situation and adapt accordingly.

FEATURES & BENEFITS

Regardless if your presentation is delivered by phone or in person, the content of your presentation remains the same. The majority of your presentation should be spent covering features and benefits.

You need to explain the features of what you are selling and how each feature will directly benefit your prospect. The features are the facts that describe your product, service, or company. Features may include circulation, materials, ingredients, speed, technology, support, skills, or warranty. *Prospects don't buy features!* The sooner you understand that concept, the more successful you will be at sales. If the message in your presentation focuses only on features, then you will be disappointed in the results. Every feature that you mention in your presentation must be tied directly to a *benefit*. You need to understand how that feature specifically benefits your prospect and then explain it to them. Without benefits, their needs are not satisfied and there is no sale.

The benefits that you are offering should address your prospect's immediate and future needs, both conscious and subconscious. Ask probing questions to identify their current and anticipated needs. Once you have a clear understanding of their situation, explain the features of what you are selling and how each feature will directly and specifically benefit their current or future needs. This shows that you listen, you understand their unique needs, and that you have a solution tailored to them. They will buy that solution of benefits because it has real *value* to them.

> *"Features must be linked to benefits. It's a standard sales component, but the feature-and-benefit connection bears repeating and reminding. Features are common, but benefits are personal and specific...Discover your prospect's 'prime desires' and personalize the benefits to him or her. Describe the end results of the transaction and how it will improve the life of your prospect...A good salesperson realizes that buyers buy solutions and results; they do not buy products or services. Know the specific aspects of your products or services that will create your client's desired result."*
>
> Jonathan Farrington
> CEO of Top Sales Associates
> Chairman of The Sales Corporation

Examples of tying features to benefits are shown below:

- Our snacks and granola bars are made from all natural organic ingredients (feature). This will help you to attract the health conscious customers in San Francisco to your store, who will also spend money on your organic coffees. Offering our organic snacks will not only increase sales from your current customers, but will also help to attract new customers to your business (benefit).

- Our publication is distributed to 50,000 affluent young professionals in Boston each month (feature). This circulation provides you with the opportunity to promote your store directly to your target audience at their homes each and every month. Through repetition and special offers in your ad, you will attract new customers and increase your business from this target audience (benefit).

- All of our assembly machines come with a five year warranty and twenty four hour technical support (feature). This means that you will never again have to worry about losing productivity when one of your machines malfunctions or goes offline. Just a quick call to our tech support line and your production will be back on track, ensuring that time and money is not lost (benefit).

"The simplest and hardest thing in sales is to remember that a prospect's primary question is 'What's in it for me?' Everything you communicate in discussion and in writing must focus on answering this question. Your success as a sales person or influencer rests squarely on your ability to put yourself in your prospect's shoes, to understand their problems, connect with

them on their level, and provide a solution that meets their needs precisely.”

David C. Miller, PCC
CEO of Business Growth Strategies

Q&A SESSIONS

Most sales presentations include a question and answer ("Q&A") session. It's an opportunity for the prospect to ask you questions and for you to provide answers. Do not rush through this session, pretend that it is not important, or make the mistake of not considering it part of the sales presentation. In most cases, this is the most important part of the sales presentation and should occupy the most amount of time. The questions asked and how your handle them could make or break the sale.

If you are presenting in person, look your prospect in the eyes, refrain from taking notes, and show that you are genuinely interested in what they are asking you. Listen closely and attentively when the prospect is asking you questions. Don't just listen to the words being spoken. Instead, identify the true meaning behind the question. The prospect is not asking a question about your product because they want to truly understand the science behind it. They are asking to understand *how it will benefit them.* Your answers need to reflect that and should always include a benefit. Do not make the amateur mistake of hearing questions about features and simply answering them by explaining the feature. In sales, every feature must be tied directly to a benefit. Therefore, the question being asked about the feature is actually about the *benefit* and must be answered with a strong and compelling benefit statement.

Anticipate the questions your prospect will ask and be prepared with answers. Brainstorm with your colleagues that have presented the same product or service many more times than you and ask for their advice. Chances are, they have probably heard all of the possible questions before and can provide you with advice on the best answers. Avoid sounding scripted with canned answers though. You still need to listen closely to each and every question and formulate an answer specific to the individual situation and prospect. Answer the questions with honesty, professionalism, and confidence. If you don't know the answer or are unsure of the best way to answer if it may appear negative, then inform the prospect confidently that you don't have the answer, but that you will get it for them soon.

> "It's been said that in order to truly be successful at selling something, you need to thoroughly understand it, articulate its benefits, and know its shortcomings. It's a lot of pressure. Here's a secret: no one expects you to know everything. It took me a long time to figure that out. I spent a lot of years fumbling through client meetings, trying to look like I knew every technical aspect of every product I sold. And while I was always very well prepared, I was not confident enough to realize that there is always some risk of weakness - some sort of exposure. Simply put, you never know exactly how a client meeting will roll. It helps to remember that a curve ball can come any time. Have a canned response ready to go for those isolated instances where you truly don't have the answer, such as, 'I'm glad you

raised that question. I'll confer will my colleagues at
corporate and get back to you by the end of the day."
Alicia Shevetone
President and Founder of Sales Concierge

Give everyone participating on the prospect side an opportunity to ask questions. This is your prospect's chance to clear up any uncertainties they may have or voice any concerns. If these concerns don't come to the surface now, they may very well be the sole reason your prospect doesn't buy from you later. It is to your advantage to proactively invite and address any concerns to avoid any surprises or delays later in the process.

SCHEDULING PRESENTATIONS

Regardless of the type of presentation, they are always most effective if scheduled in advance. This shows respect for your prospect's schedule and ensures that both parties allocate enough time to focus on the sales presentation. Schedule the presentation when it is convenient for the prospect and then send a confirmation email one day before to remind the prospect of the schedule commitment. Although this method is preferred, not all sales presentations can be scheduled in advance. A cold call or follow up call in the sales process can easily turn into a full sales presentation if the timing is right. For some sales cycles, a scheduled sales presentation may not be necessary or applicable. For those reasons, you need to be ready at all times to jump into presentation mode and perform.

PRICING

It doesn't matter if you are selling a product or a service, if you are in outside sales or inside sales, or if your sales cycle is long and relationship driven or short and transactional. It doesn't matter how many competitors you have, how big your territory is, or what industry you do business in. As long as you are in sales and selling something, then price is part of your sales process. If there were no prices, then money would not be exchanged, commissions would not be paid, and we would all be in the charity business of just giving things away. That is obviously not the case. Our economy is built around the value of money and exchanging money for products, services, housing, medicine, education, etc. Everything costs something. What you are selling obviously costs something and it has a price. How you feel about that price and how you present it to your prospect is a crucial part of closing each deal.

Do not make the mistake of thinking that price is the deciding factor in every sale. Rarely will a prospect make a purchasing decision based solely on price. In most cases, the quality, dependability, style, size, technology, materials, or warranty are more important to the prospect than the price. Most prospects would rather pay more for something that meets their needs, than pay less and get something that does not meet their needs. Prospects buy to satisfy their needs or solve problems. Prospects buy products and services that provide them with benefits and value. *Prospects do not buy price!* If you can understand this theory and use it to your advantage in sales, then price will rarely be an issue.

There is a reason that the pricing chapter comes after the cold calling and presentations chapters of this book. That is the order in which pricing should be discussed in the sales process! You need to identify decision makers first, uncover their needs, and explain how your product or service can satisfy those needs using features and benefits. You need to create *value* in what you are selling by explaining to your prospects why they need your product or service. Once they realize that they need what you are selling, they truly want it, and they understand the value, then price becomes secondary. They are buying on value and as long as the price is within their budget, then the sale is closed. There will be no need to offer discounts or negotiate pricing. They understand the value and they are willing to pay full price to get that value.

> *"If you can't price your value, all your customer will see is your cost, and customers don't buy on cost. Customer Value = Benefit / Cost. The greater the benefit, the greater the value, and cost becomes a non-issue."*
> *Stu Schlackman*
> *President of Competitive Excellence*

Believe in yourself and the value of what you are selling. Do not do yourself a disservice by always discounting your prices or asking your sales manager for a special deal "just this one time". If you use that crutch once, you will eventually depend on it and use it whenever the sales process becomes tough. Instead, stand by your price and use other sales strategies to overcome the price objection to close the deal. Is price really the true objection? Did you do a good job of explaining the *benefits* (not just the features) and creating *value*? Did you establish credibility and create urgency? Ask yourself those questions and revisit the parts of the sales process that might need to be improved upon before dropping the price. Dropping the price without answering those questions may still not result in a sale. The prospect may perceive the new lower price as a sign that you were trying to overcharge them to begin with and are not a trustworthy or ethical business person. If the lower price does incent the prospect to buy, chances are it will be a short term business relationship because there is no perceived value and they will switch vendors as soon as a lower price is presented to them by someone else. Keep in mind also, that the lower the price, the lower your commission. Not only are you devaluing your product with a lower price, but you are also devaluing your time with a lower paycheck.

> *"Don't whine about price. Rather, believe in the value of what you sell and sell the value. If you don't believe in the value of what you sell, neither will your prospect. If you're always asking your sales manager for a better price, you're not doing your job, which is to sell value, not price. Price will always be a factor in every sale, but is rarely the deciding factor."*
>
> *Brian Jeffrey*
> *President of Salesforce Assessment Ltd*

> *"Perception is the key to your success in this crazy business. Your appeal as a salesperson depends upon the*

*client's perception of what you bring to the table. As
soon as you offer to lower your price, you can be sure
that the client's perception is going to dwindle."*

Ed Brodow
Author of "Negotiation Boot Camp"

This does not mean that you can never lower your prices during the sales process. When competing for a large account, it is normal to have a few rounds of bids while the pool of vendors is narrowed down and decisions are made. This does not mean that you have to bid the lowest price to win the business, as the decision will ultimately still be based on value. They will expect to see some downward movement nevertheless, so build in enough wiggle room on your first bid to allow for discounts throughout the sales process. In addition to bidding for large accounts, it is customary in some industries for sales professionals to negotiate price on almost every sale. If you are selling cars or houses, negotiating price will be a major part of almost every deal you close. Even in these instances though, keep in mind that prospects will make their final buying decision based on value, not price. If you sell on price alone, you will close less deals and have a higher turnover of customers. Believe in your prices and sell value.

"In any sale, if you want to have a competitive advantage, be there first and lead with value. A compelling value proposition that is stating the added value a specific customer's key contact can get, by using some of your capabilities, is your most powerful tool."

Jean Giannelli
Managing Partner at SmartServices Network

PRICE VS. PROFIT

Keep in mind that the price in question for the sale you are trying to close does not just affect you and the prospect. The price ultimately affects the profits of the company you work for, which in turn affects every employee, department, and budget. Lowering the price by 20% may help you close the deal, but does it hurt the business? Does that 20% discount erode profits and actually end up costing the company money instead of making money? In many cases, you will not receive your full commission (or any commission) or be eligible for bonuses on deals that do not meet the company's defined profit model. In these cases, was it worth it to lower the price to close the deal, if you and your company don't make any money on it? Be aware of the bottom line and the profit margin when negotiating prices. Ensure that all of your deals are always profitable for you and your company. Your job and your paycheck may depend on it.

> *"You are not being paid to make sales. You're being paid to make money. Understand the concept of profit and gross margins. That's what you're selling. As a salesperson, you are running your own independent business under the umbrella of your employer. Run it profitably."*
>
> *Brian Jeffrey*
> *President of Salesforce Assessment Ltd*

CLOSING

Closing the sale - it's the most important step in the sales process and really is all that matters. You can have the most aggressive prospecting list, make the most sales calls of anyone in your company, deliver the most engaging presentations, and create the most professional proposals, but none of that matters if you aren't good at closing deals. Without a close, there is no sale. Without a sale, there is no commission (and no job) for you. It's like getting a hole in one in golf or throwing a strike in bowling, but then losing at the end to your opponent. In the end, only the final score and the winner matters. The same is true in sales. Your sales manager may monitor your call volume and ask to discuss your leads and your sales funnel, but in the end it all comes down to results. Were you able to close the deal before it got cold or before your competitor stole the business? How many sales did you close in a given period? Did you meet your sales quota or goal? Everything that you have read up until now in this book builds up to the close. If you follow the advice, do everything correctly in the sales process, identify needs, focus on benefits, create value, and overcome objections, then closing the deal is easy.

> *"If you have really qualified how working with you and your products will solve the prospect's problem or make their job easier, then buying from you is the next*

logical step for them to take. Closing is difficult when
the prospect isn't convinced you're the best choice."

Lynn Hidy
Founder of UpYourTeleSales.com

There are no secrets to closing deals. Closing is not a scary or complicated process. It's as simple as asking for the business. If you don't ask for the sale, you won't get it! The customer knows that you are salesperson and that you are there to sell to them, so they are expecting it. Don't let them down! Establish credibility with your prospect, identify their needs, explain how your product will benefit them and satisfy their needs, overcome any objections they may have, and then simply ask for the sale. If you did your job and created value, then they already want what you are selling and the answer is simple. You want to sell to them and they want to buy from you. Ask for the sale and be confident that the answer will be yes.

There is a difference between sales professionals and order takers. An order taker waits for the prospect to tell them what, when, and how much they want to buy, and then simply processes the order. That is not "sales" and there are no sales skills required to be an order taker. There is also very little money to be made if you are just taking orders. In contrast, sales professionals *proactively* make deals happen by aggressively seeking out business, moving prospects through the sales process, and closing deals. They don't wait for the prospect to ask to buy. They satisfy needs, create urgency, and *ask for the business*. They don't let the prospect tell them what they want to buy and how much of it. Sales professionals make a recommendation based on the prospects' needs, and then back it up with a recommendation at the stated price as the best decision and the best value.

ASSUMPTIVE CLOSE

There are several different strategies that can be used when closing a sale. One of the most effective strategies is an "assumptive close". Using this method, you *assume* that the deal is done and speak to the prospect as if the sale was already closed. Without actually asking for the sale or having the prospect say "yes", you are discussing plans with the prospect as if they are already a client! This may involve scheduling a delivery, discussing ad copy, introducing them to their customer service rep, or finalizing billing information. This method is used when you feel confident that the prospect is ready to buy. You'll probably still need to have an agreement signed to officially close the deal, but by then it is really just a formality. The client is already assuming the role of a client and moving forward through the assumptive close method.

TRIAL CLOSE

A trial close is a different strategy that should be used when you are having difficulty reading the prospect and judging their readiness to buy. It can be used throughout the sales process to gauge interest levels. This method allows you to try the close by asking qualifying questions. Ask the prospect questions that include "if you were to move forward..."or "if I were able to revise the proposal to include..." Their reaction and answers to the trial close questions will identify their readiness to buy and prepare you for the close.

ACCOUNT MANAGEMENT

Even if your organization has a customer service team that takes care of clients, *you* are still ultimately responsible for *your clients*. These clients made a decision to start a business relationship with your organization based on your influence. They know you and they trust you. You have a professional and moral obligation to these clients to ensure that they receive excellent service after the sale is closed. This involves checking in with your clients periodically to ensure that they are satisfied. It also involves keeping an open line of communication with anyone in your organization that interacts with your clients (customer service, accounting, shipping, tech support, design, etc.) to ensure that there are no issues.

You work hard to close deals and obtain new clients. It takes a lot of time and effort to identify new prospects, generate interest, present your product, overcome objections, create proposals, close deals, and complete the necessary paperwork. Protect the investment you have already made in your business by ensuring you retain those clients. In many organizations, new clients are turned over to another department to ship the orders, design the ads, collect the cash, or provide customer service, tech support, or installation services. Keep in mind that your coworkers in those other departments are paid an hourly wage or salary that is not dependant on your clients. They are paid the same if your clients are happy or not. Your commission paycheck is the only paycheck that is affected by your clients' satisfaction. If one of your clients decides to take their business to your competitor due to an issue with another department in your company, it is *your* problem. *Your client* is gone and with them goes *your commission.* Your future commissions depend on your current clients being happy and receiving excellent service. Protect your clients and your income through proactive communication on all levels. This is not to suggest that your colleagues don't care about your clients or that you can't trust them. That is obviously not true, as you are all on the same team. It just means that you have a more vested interest in your clients due to the fact that your compensation is directly tied to them. Look out for yourself and protect your income.

REPEAT BUSINESS

The easiest sales you will ever make are to your *existing clients*! If you are selling a product that has a shelf life, then you should stay in touch with your clients to ensure they reorder once that product expires or is consumed. If you are selling a service that needs to be renewed every year, then staying in touch with your clients throughout the year will make the renewal easy. If the product met their needs and they received excellent customer service, then the renewal is the next logical step. Renewals of services or reorders of products are *sales*. In many cases, those sales are recognized the same way as sales to new clients and commissions are paid the same way. They are valuable and easy sales!

The strength of your relationships and the amount of communication that you have with your clients will directly effect your ability to solidify future renewals or reorders from those clients. If you simply sell a service to a client in May, go a whole year without speaking to them, and then call them next May for the renewal, you may have a difficult time renewing. A lot could have changed in that year that you are not aware of and not prepared for. Your contact could be replaced with another decision maker who does not know you and you may have to start from scratch. The client's business may have changed drastically and your service may no longer meet their needs. The client might have had an issue with an aspect of the service in December that was not resolved. Instead of you being aware and getting involved to help fix the issue, your client has been entertaining bids from your competitors for the past three months and it's now too late for you. All of these scenarios will make it more difficult to renew the business with your client. They could all have been avoided if you built a strong relationship and maintained periodic communication with your client. If you had called them in December, you would have learned about that problem, fixed it, kept the client happy, and prevented your competitors from getting their foot in the door. If you spoke with your client on a regular basis, you would have known that their business changed and you could have recommended a more appropriate service to meet their needs. You would also have known that the decision makers were changing and had an opportunity to introduce yourself and welcome the new person in the beginning before your competition did.

Client communication and building strong relationships with your clients are necessary to ensure future business. Your clients are your *assets* and they need to be protected and cared for. Make the time to invest into your clients. It's as simple as scheduling periodic reminders in your CRM or Outlook to just send them a short email or give them a quick call. Stop in to see them periodically or schedule a visit once per year to get some valuable face time. Send them a thank you card whenever they sign agreements and include them on your holiday card list. These actions don't require a lot of effort or time, but the impact they have on your clients (and your paychecks) will be well worth it.

UP-SELLING

In addition to generating repeat business from your clients, you may also be able to increase the existing business with up-sells. This is accomplished by selling more to the client than they originally purchased. An example would be an advertising campaign that you originally sold as a quarter-page black and white ad for one year. After speaking with the client on a regular basis, building the relationship, earning their trust, and showing them the positive results, you are able to confidently recommend moving their quarter-page ad to a premium position in color for the remainder of the campaign. The result would be a seventy percent increase in monthly revenue and the difference in annual revenue would be recorded as an up-sell. Other up-sell examples include adding an extended warranty, including product upgrades, increasing the quantity of products shipped monthly, or adding additional services from your company to their current program.

Any additional revenue that you can obtain from a current client is considered an up-sell. Up-sells and renewals with current clients are easy sales and a smart use of your time. Take advantage of these opportunities to increase revenue from your current clients. The more clients you have, the more up-sell opportunities you will have, and the more money you will make. Don't be an "order taker" and wait for your clients to contact you and buy more. You may be waiting a long time, as they may not be aware that other opportunities exist. Instead, be their consultant by making proactive and professional recommendations that will benefit the client. Pay attention to their changing business needs and make recommendations to meet those needs. As their business grows, make recommendations that will grow with them and allow your revenue from them to grow as well. As your company launches new products or services, reach out to your current clients to introduce them to these new opportunities. Selling a new service to a current client will be much easier than selling a new service to a new prospect. Take advantage of the clients and relationships you already have to grow your business smartly.

Up-sells are only possible if you have gained your clients' trust and confidence. This is achieved through proactive communication, building a strong relationship, acting as their partner, and making the right recommendations with their best interests in mind. Start by treating them fairly and only recommending products or services that you know will benefit them. Then, follow up on every sale with your clients to measure their satisfaction and discuss the results or impact it created for them. Resolve any issues expeditiously and go out of your way to ensure they receive excellent customer service and that every detail is taken care of. Your clients will notice and appreciate this attention. They'll view you as a partner and know that you genuinely care about their business. They will trust you and will buy anything from you. If the products that you recommended in the past worked for them and helped their business, then buying additional products from you will be no problem. You will also find that these clients will remain loyal to you and may even follow you to other companies that you or they move on to in the future. If you treat them right and take care of them, they will trust you, and you will have those clients for life.

> *"Follow up to ensure the solution is delivering the desired results. Leverage those results to gain more business with that client."*
>
> *David R. Barnes Jr.*
> *Managing Partner, Result Driven Consulting Group*

WORDS OF WISDOM

" It's often thought that the reason to enter the sales profession is money. Yet, if money is your core focus, you will find all of your prospects develop a limp - as they walk away from you while they cover their wallets. A better word to focus your selling career upon is matchmaker. On one side, you have a supplier that offers products, services, or technology. On the other side, you have buyers with needs, desires, and challenges. Your core role is to put the buyer together with the supplier - the matchmaker. To do this effectively, you have to develop mastery of both so you can identify synergies between these two entities. Focus your career on being the matchmaker and the money takes care of itself."

Lee B. Salz
Sales Management Strategist of Sales Architects

"Take the word 'selling' out of your vocabulary. Insert the phrase 'solution provider'. In today's hyper-speed global economy only companies and individuals that provide near perfect solutions, that can produce the desired return on investment, will be successful."

David R. Barnes Jr.
Managing Partner of Result Driven Consulting Group

"Focus on gaining a 'customer for life' versus a sale and ensure your sales process and philosophy support this."

Tessa Stowe
Owner of SalesConversation.com

"Stop selling your product and start helping your customers to be more successful in their business."

Steve Gielda

Principal of Ignite Selling, Inc.

"Selling has nothing (and I mean nothing) to do with you. It's helping your customers grow and reach their targets. It's the one and only way to reach (and over perform) your targets. When you adapt this attitude into your life, you never have to cold call again."

Arno Diepeveen

xSELLerator of Arno & Company

"A true sales professional is an expert at persuading others to do what is in their best interests. When the sales professional puts others' needs ahead of their own, they always win in the long run."

Rollis Fontenot III

Author of "Go Out and Sell Something!"

"The more you sell, the less the client trusts you to tell them the truth. The more you sell, the less inclined the client is to listen. The more you sell, the more you tend to look (and act) like a hammer looking for a nail, where any nail will do. In reality, the more you sell, the less you win."

Peter Bourke

Principal of Better Way Sales Strategies

"The most powerful people in the world are those that can sell. My advice to you is because you have this power, and will ultimately be trusted, you have an obligation to your target audience that you will promote and sell with authenticity, integrity, and ethics. That way when you are true to yourself, you will speak with such passion that they will know you have their best interest in mind, and it won' be selling, it will be helping."

Tracy Repchuk
Speaker and Author of "31 Days to Millionaire Marketing Miracles"

"It is our duty, as noble knights of the selling profession, to keep honor in the game. True salespeople are not cheaters, not liars, and not manipulators. They are listeners, they are givers, and they are more concerned with putting the needs of the many in front of their own."

Carson Heady
Author of "Birth of a Salesman"

"Injecting fun into your business is the single most powerful, yet least understood, competitive advantage available today. Being fun to do business with provides you with a distinct competitive advantage over your direct competitors. Why? All things being equal, most people will chose to deal with someone who is fun to do business with. All things not being equal, people would still rather deal with someone who is fun to do business with. The moment your customers start perceiving you as being fun to do business with, your company will rapidly start out-selling, out-marketing, and out-performing the competition."

Bill Todd
President and CEO of Immediate Impact Marketing

"Sell something that you are passionate about or believe strongly in. Don't just settle for a paycheck! Remember - if you wouldn't buy it, you can't sell it."

John Boyens
Co-Founder and President of Boyens Group

"The best sales tool you will ever possess is self-confidence. It comes from within, it can't be feigned, and there is simply no substitute for it."

Jeff Davidson
Author, Speaker, and "Work-Life Balance Expert"

"Shortcuts in sales can lead to dead ends. Follow the steps of the sales process for success."

John Gomes
VP of Marketing & New Business Development at Atrium Medical

"Selling is a business of failure. A closing rate of 30% means a failure rate of 70%. Every 'no' gets you one step closer to a 'yes'."

Brian Jeffrey
President of Salesforce Assessment Ltd

"It is vital to understand the kind of person you are. It will define the kind of sales to which you will be best suited. If you're into building relationships, then work in a consultative sales environment. Conversely, if you're driven by targets, then transactional sales is the place for you. Understanding this early in your career will save you hours/days/years of frustration and set you up for long-term success."

Helen Blake
Director of Futurecurve

"Always tell people what they need to know, not what you think they want to hear. Integrity is one of the cornerstones of effective relationship oriented selling behaviors. Without credibility, there is no trust. Without trust, there is no business relationship.

When your customers ask for information, give them the facts and the unfiltered truth. Your credibility is at stake."

Dave Cooke
CEO and Founder of Strategic Resource Group, LLC

"Always sell to people. This may seem obvious, but it cannot be emphasized enough. You are not selling to an organization or to a conglomerate, but to actual, real people. It is important to remember that all people are different, so you cannot sell the same way to everyone. Second, no two sales are the same, even if they are made to the same company under similar circumstances. To be a good salesperson, it isn't enough to know how to sell. You must aim to become a people expert. It may sound shocking, but the best professional salespeople actually like people! Remember, people buy from people - they always will."

Jonathan Farrington
CEO of Top Sales Associates
Chairman of The Sales Corporation

"I believe that society is experiencing yet another major, social paradigm shift - that people are once again appreciating the value of caring and trusting 'interpersonal relations' in both the corporate world and the marketplace. I maintain that 'people still buy people,' and they buy best from people who treat them like they matter. I teach that successful selling is not only about closing the sale, it's about building quality relationships, rich connections, and loyal trust - first with yourself, and then with your customers."

Diane Marie Pinkard
Author & Trainer of Sales Success with Happiness & Heart

"Never forget a customer. Never let a customer forget you."

Hank Trisler

Supreme Commander of The Trisler Company, Inc.

Author of "No Bull Selling" and "No Bull Sales Management"

"The quality of your clients will be determined by the quality of your relationships."

Dr. Richard Norris

Self-leadership and Performance Coach at Serendipity Global Ltd.

"Feelings are not facts. Sales is a very predictable profession when you know your facts - your numbers. Keep accurate records of calls made, appointments set, and closings made. When you know what it takes to make one sale, you can make as many sales as you want."

Donald E. Wetmore

President of Productivity Institute

"Selling is 90% science and 10% art. Have a plan for every sale and follow it as best you can. The rest is the art."

Dave Stein

CEO and Founder of ES Research Group, Inc.

"We all have talents. We all have shortcomings. One of the most delicate tricks to life is to keep balance in our focus and not let those shortcomings define us or overtake what we are passionate about or good at."

Carson Heady

Author of "Birth of a Salesman"

ACKNOWLEDGEMENTS

I would like to sincerely thank all of the people that helped to make this book possible and that have positively impacted my career.

Thank you to all of the contributing authors that voluntarily provided quotes for this book. Your comments strengthen my message and add tremendous value to the readers. I appreciate your willingness to help with this important project and influence the next generation of sales professionals.

To John Gomes, thank you for all of your valuable feedback and advice. I appreciate your time and your insight. Thank you to Jack Webber for teaching, inspiring, and mentoring me when I started my sales career. Thank you to Eric Goodwin for trusting me, challenging me, and empowering me with an important role within your organization.

To my parents, Ron and Paulette, thank you for providing me with an excellent education and a strong foundation to build my career upon. I am grateful for all that you have done for me.

This book and my career would not be possible without the strong support of my wife, Stephanie. Thank you for confidently standing by me and always believing in me. I truly appreciate all of your support and understanding. I also value all of your patience, feedback, and help with this book.

Thank you,
Brian Calderone

ABOUT THE AUTHOR

B rian Calderone has experienced a successful sales career selling advertising campaigns and hospitality services, along with managing a national sales force and owning an online advertising business. He has a bachelor's degree in Marketing Communications and Advertising.

BrianCalderone@gmail.com

Made in the USA
Charleston, SC
13 January 2014